Verna Meyer's Menu Cookbook

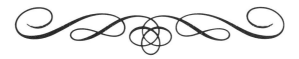

Verna Meyer's Menu Cookbook

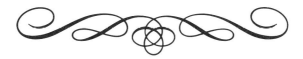

Dining at Home in Style

by Verna E. Meyer

DILLON PRESS, INC. MINNEAPOLIS, MINNESOTA 55415

Table setting and cover photo courtesy of Dayton's.

Dillon Press, Inc., 500 South Third Street
Minneapolis, Minnesota 55415

Printed in the United States of America

Library of Congress Cataloging in Publication Data

Meyer, Verna E.   1895-
  Verna Meyer's Menu cookbook.

  Includes index.
  1. Cookery. 2. Menus. I. Title. II. Title: Menu cookbook.
TX715.M624   641.5   80-19120
ISBN 0-87518-199-6

I wish to dedicate this book to the members of La Société de la Cuisine Française des Amis de V.E.M., many of whom have helped to compile this material, and to all of my students who have followed my cooking principles for so many years.

I would like to thank my special assistants, Eleanor Chinn and Barbara Perrenoud, for giving so generously of their time and talents in helping to put this book together. Theirs has been a labor of love involving countless hours of testing, tasting, talking and typing. Without them this book would not exist.

My thanks also go to Elizabeth Kaibel for her invaluable assistance in editing, and to her and Elizabeth Donaldson for their help in presenting the introductory remarks for each menu.

Contents

Foreword

Not so long ago, at a reception for Robert Carrier, Food and Drink Editor of *House Beautiful*, the host rose, gave a toast, and said, "Without Verna Meyer, most of us would not be meeting here tonight!"

She is the *grande dame* of cooking schools and classes in the Twin Cities of Minneapolis and Saint Paul. Mention other cooking schools and teachers, and you will hear compliments. Mention Verna Meyer, and there is reverence. The others—most of them—are her alumni.

Verna Meyer has a string of culinary honors behind her name; among them is the coveted Diploma of the International Wine and Food Society. She has been teaching cooking—focusing on the French style—since 1943, and it is said that Verna Meyer took up where Escoffier stopped.

She has advised master chefs on banquets and other culinary bashes, including inaugural dinners for Minnesota governors and visiting dignitaries. But it is in the family kitchen that she excels, taking simple, ordinary foods and making posh meals of them.

A longtime advocate of fresh foods and sound nutrition, Verna is a little wary of the "newness" of the Nouvelle Cuisine. "I've always espoused the philosophy of half as much being twice as good," she says. Her conviction is incarnate in menus of studied simplicity in which each entry sets off its companions to perfection.

Now in her eighty-fifth year, Verna has relinquished the demanding regimen of the daily cooking school in favor of special classes for her prized students. Having brought them through all levels of cooking, French and American, she now guides them through the cuisines of the Orient, Russia, Spain, Italy, Hungary, and Germany.

Here is her own carefully researched and tested cookbook—thirty-seven years of cooking with Verna Meyer.

GARETH D. HIEBERT
Oliver Towne Columnist
St. Paul Dispatch
Saint Paul, Minnesota

Introduction

This book began almost forty years ago, when I taught my first cooking class. Since then a great many of the hundreds of men and women who have been my students have asked that I collect my recipes—and thoughts—in some permanent form.

For a long time I resisted the idea, believing that fine cooking involves too many intangibles, immeasurables, and instincts to be set down in writing. I still believe that. But I have also come to realize that a good cookbook can be not only a source of inspiration to its readers, but a lasting forum for a teacher wishing to share all that is unique about his or her methods.

In that sense this book is a summation of my career in the classroom. If you have never taken one of my courses, I hope that this book will give you a taste of the excitement, and ease, of cooking the Meyer way. If you have been one of my students, I trust that it will serve as a valuable supplement to your classwork. In either case, I hope that this book will make you want to go into the kitchen and cook.

Cooking in the United States has undergone a revolution since I taught my first class in nutrition during World War II. Americans who fifteen years ago did not know quiche from quenelles now think nothing of turning out everything from Coquilles Saint-Jacques to Fettucine Alfredo in their own homes. Wine sales have risen faster than a soufflé in a hot oven. Accordingly you will find that this book assumes a basic level of cooking knowledge and skills on the part of its readers, although anyone who follows the instructions should easily be able to prepare all the recipes here.

The menus in this book are divided into five sections: Breakfasts, Luncheons, Dinners, Suppers and Informal Entertaining, and Foreign Specialties. With the exception of the breakfasts, most are three-course meals and wines are specified as appropriate. In some cases I have suggested broad classifications so that you may choose a compatible wine according to the varieties offered in your area. Coffees and teas have been mentioned only if a specific type would be especially suitable. Similarly, I have included recipes for breads only if a particular one is important to the menu.

You should, of course, feel free to make additions or substitutions whenever whim or circumstances dictate. In particular, I have always urged my students to use fresh foods in season and I encourage you to do the same. Don't hesitate to substitute when one of nature's gifts, such as asparagus, is in its prime. You will find that changing your menus to correspond with the changes in temperature greatly enhances your appreciation of the wonders of each season.

You will find an extensive basics section in the back of the book. Basics includes elementary recipes for the standard dishes—sauces, breads, salad dressings, and so forth—that are essential to any good cook's repertoire. Although there are references to these recipes throughout the book, you will undoubtedly find yourself using them on your own in daily meal planning and preparation. It is my hope that you will come to regard Basics as your kitchen "Book Friday."

Creating a special dinner, sharing a glass of wine with one's friends, nourishing a child with good homemade food—these are among life's great pleasures. As a teacher, it has been my privilege to share with students my techniques, principles, enthusiasms, and prejudices concerning cooking. It has been my goal to touch each of their lives in some small way, if only by imparting some of the fun and satisfaction to be gained from preparing fine food. I hope that, in a similar way, this book will touch your life too.

Breakfasts

A Continental Breakfast

FRUIT PLATTER

BRIOCHE   A TRIO OF PRESERVES

To those who have traveled in Europe, a continental breakfast conjures up images of crusty French bread or flaky croissants, sweet butter, and *café au lait* enjoyed in one's hotel room before setting out to see the sights of Paris. But what we have here is *un petit déjeuner* of a higher order: nothing less than brioche, the incomparably rich French egg bread, accompanied by colorful pots of preserves and an artfully arranged mosaic of fresh fruit slices. One whiff and you'll be transported to the Champs Élysées.

FRUIT PLATTER

Honeydew melon
Cantaloupe
Mangoes
Papayas
Kiwi fruits
Seedless green grapes

Select a large platter and arrange the melons, cut in quarters or eighths, fairly evenly around the edge. Slice the mangoes and papaya; peel the kiwi and cut into coins. Pile the slices among the melon wedges as decoratively as possible. Roll the grapes in sugar and scatter over the fruit arrangement. You may add or substitute any fruit that happens to be in season. I have suggested these particular fruits because they are generally available throughout the year.

BRIOCHE

1½	**packages dry yeast**
¼	**cup warm water (105°-115°)**
2	**whole eggs**
2	**egg yolks**
3	**tablespoons sugar**
1	**teaspoon salt**
¼	**cup hot water**
½	**cup butter**
2	**tablespoons dry milk**
1¼	**cups all-purpose flour**
1¼	**cups cake flour**

Dissolve the yeast in the ¼ cup warm water, adding a few grains of sugar. In a large bowl, beat the eggs and egg yolks together until light. Add the sugar and salt, mixing well. Pour the ¼ cup hot water over the butter to melt it and add to the egg mixture, along with the dry milk. Stir in the yeast and then the two flours. Beat well, cover the bowl, and let rise until double in a warm place.

Preheat oven to 400°. Generously grease about 12 to 14 brioche molds, custard cups, or cups of muffin tins.

Beat the dough with a wooden spoon. Fill the molds half full, place in a warm place, cover, and let rise until double. Bake about 15 minutes, or until the brioches are browned on top and test done with a cake tester.

If desired, the brioches may be baked in small loaves. The loaves slice and toast well, and they may also be served with jam for tea. Individual brioches are used for breakfasts and luncheons. Stale brioche makes a divine bread pudding.

A TRIO OF PRESERVES

Choose your favorite high quality preserves, jams, and marmalades, making an effort to have a variety of colors and flavors, such as strawberry, peach, orange or pineapple, and blueberry or black raspberry. Present them in pretty pots.

Breakfast with a Flair

TOMATO COCKTAIL

FRENCH OMELET

ENGLISH MUFFINS   BLUEBERRY CONSERVE

There is nothing more delectable, more perfectly pleasing to both the eye and the palate than a puffed and golden French omelet. Transcendent in their simplicity and versatility, omelets are remarkably easy to prepare if one takes care to acquire the freshest possible ingredients and proper pan. Master the technique described below and you will find yourself turning out a matchless omelet in less than a minute. Guests waiting for theirs to slide out of the pan can sip a zesty tomato cocktail or slather some oh-so-good blueberry conserve on your homemade English muffins. Is there a better way to start the day?

TOMATO COCKTAIL

1   46-ounce can tomato juice
3   sprigs parsley
2   ribs celery, roughly chopped
1   teaspoon Worcestershire sauce
1   teaspoon horseradish
    Juice of ½ lemon
½   teaspoon paprika
½   cup crushed ice
    Lemon slices
    Fresh basil leaves or tiny parsley sprigs

In blender or food processor, place 1 cup of the tomato juice, the parsley, celery, Worcestershire sauce, horseradish, lemon juice, and paprika. Blend until well combined. Pour into a pitcher and add the remaining tomato juice and the crushed ice. Chill.

To serve, garnish each serving with a slice of lemon and a leaf of basil or a tiny parsley sprig and a little more crushed ice. Serves 8.

FRENCH OMELETS

To be authentic, each omelet must be made individually. Therefore, the ingredients and directions below are for one omelet. Multiply the ingredients by the number of servings you desire, pouring just enough into the pan each time to cook one omelet.

3   eggs
1   teaspoon water
    Dash salt
1   tablespoon cold butter

Lightly beat the eggs, water, and salt with a fork until they are just mixed. Do not overbeat. Heat the omelet pan until a drop of water will dance on its surface. Drop in the butter and swirl it around the pan with a fork to grease the entire surface. When the butter is sizzling but before it begins to brown, add the eggs. As they cook on the bottom and sides, use a fork to pull the eggs away from the edge of the pan toward the center, letting the uncooked eggs roll to the sides, turning and tilting the pan as necessary. When the eggs have lost their gloss but are not quite set on top, turn out onto the plate, folding the second half of the omelet over the first half as it slides out of the pan. Serve plain or use any of the variations below.

Fines herbes: Add a pinch each of tarragon, parsley, chervil, and chives to the eggs before cooking the omelet.

Curried mushroom: Drain one 4-ounce can mushrooms, reserving the liquid. Sauté the mushrooms in butter 2 minutes and remove from the pan. Add enough butter to make 2 tablespoons. Add ½ teaspoon curry powder and stir and cook 1 minute. Then add 2 tablespoons flour and stir to make a roux. Add enough chicken stock to the mushroom liquid to make 1 cup, and add this to the roux. Cook and stir briskly with a whisk until thickened and smooth. Season to taste with salt and white pepper. Add the mushrooms. Serve a portion over each omelet.

Chutney and sour cream: Top the omelet with a dollop of sour cream; spoon a small portion of chutney in the center of the sour cream.

ENGLISH MUFFINS

See Basics, page 182.

BLUEBERRY CONSERVE

1   cup frozen blueberries, unsweetened
½   cup sugar
    Dash nutmeg
1   teaspoon lemon juice
1   1-inch strip lemon rind

Cook all ingredients together in a small saucepan until slightly thickened. This is not a thick jam.

Breakfast
at Brennan's

MILK PUNCH

EGGS HUSSARDE   **BROILED TOMATOES**

BANANAS FOSTER   **COFFEE WITH CHICORY**

Come with us now to Brennan's, in the heart of the French Quarter in New Orleans. You'll want to start this truly unforgettable breakfast with a real eye-opener, and nothing could be more appropriate than milk punch, as southern as hominy grits and laced with just the right amount of brandy or bourbon. Proceed to Brennan's original—eggs hussarde. (The origins of the name are obscure, though most likely it refers to red-coated hussars, mercenary soldiers of the eighteenth century.) A Holland rusk is layered with Canadian bacon, sauce of the wine merchant, and a poached egg, all topped off with a tomato-tinged béarnaise sauce. *Voilà*! The spectacular finish to this meal must be tasted to be believed, but suffice it to say that bananas, warmed in a chafing dish with butter and cinnamon, are flamed with rum and poured over vanilla ice cream. Truly a regal way to end breakfast on Royal Street.

MILK PUNCH

Because milk punch should be mixed fresh for each serving, the ingredients and directions below are for one drink.

1¼ ounces bourbon or brandy
3 ounces light cream (half and half will do)
1 teaspoon sugar (superfine preferred)
⅛ teaspoon vanilla
Nutmeg

In a shaker or blender, thoroughly combine the bourbon or brandy, cream, sugar, and vanilla. Pour into an 8-ounce highball glass, add ice, and sprinkle with nutmeg.

EGGS HUSSARDE

8 eggs
White vinegar
8 slices Canadian bacon
8 Holland rusks
1 cup Sauce of the Wine Merchant
(See Basics, page 171)
1 cup Choron Sauce (See Basics, page 172)

Warm the Canadian bacon in the top of a double boiler over simmering water or in a nonstick frying pan, turning frequently, until heated through but not dry or browned.

Lightly grease individual egg poachers. Have ready a deep stainless steel, enameled, or nonstick skillet filled with water and white vinegar (1 quart water to 2½ tablespoons vinegar) to a depth of about 2 inches or enough to cover the eggs. Break eggs into the egg poachers. Lower the eggs into the skillet of barely simmering vinegar-water and poach for 4 minutes. Carefully remove eggs from holder to a towel to drain. (Poached eggs may easily be done as much as a day ahead of time. Remove the eggs from the poaching liquid and put them carefully in a bowl of cold water to stop the cooking. Store, refrigerated, in an uncovered bowl of cold water. Reheat in simmering water for 2 minutes.)

Baked eggs (see "A Midwinter Brunch," page 22) may be substituted for the poached eggs in this recipe.

Place a slice of bacon on each Holland rusk and ladle with sauce of the wine merchant. Top with an egg and a spoonful of choron sauce.

Serve with a broiled tomato half on the plate. Serves 8.

BROILED TOMATOES

4 red, ripe, flavorful tomatoes, halved
crosswise
Butter, melted
Salt
Pepper
Basil
Fresh bread crumbs

Preheat oven to 375°. Brush the tops of the tomato halves with melted butter and sprinkle with salt, pepper, and basil. Top with fresh bread crumbs. Bake for 10 minutes or until cooked but still firm. Serves 8.

BANANAS FOSTER

8 bananas, not too ripe
¼ cup butter
1 cup brown sugar
½ cup dark rum
   Cinnamon
   Cognac or rum
   Vanilla ice cream, optional

Peel the bananas and cut them in half lengthwise. In a chafing dish, combine the butter, brown sugar, dark rum, and a dash of cinnamon. Cook until sugar dissolves and syrup begins to bubble. Warm the bananas in the syrup, turning once. Warm a small amount of cognac or rum in a small pan and carefully light with a long match. While flaming, pour over the bananas; allow the flames to die out naturally. Serve immediately, with vanilla ice cream, if desired. Serves 8.

COFFEE WITH CHICORY

Dark roast coffee with chicory, traditional to New Orleans, is available in most large supermarkets. Prepare it by the drip method, making a fairly strong brew.

A Midwinter Brunch

SAUTÉED APPLES

BAKED EGGS **ENGLISH STYLE SAUSAGE**

BISCUITS **SPICED HONEY**

ENGLISH BREAKFAST TEA

The English have a way with breakfast, and this hearty brunch would certainly be most welcome on a frosty morning in Kensington. This is plain food, as at home in fashionable Knightsbridge as it would be on the table of a Yorkshire salesman. You'll find it filling, nourishing, and warming from the tips of your toes to the depths of your soul.

SAUTÉED APPLES

    4 red apples
    3 tablespoons butter
    ½ cup brown sugar
    ½ cup water

Core the apples and slice into wedges. Do not peel. In a skillet, stir the butter and brown sugar together to blend; add the water. Add apples and cook slowly, turning with a pancake turner until tender and well glazed. (A few drops of red food color may be added if desired.) Serves 6 to 8.

BAKED EGGS

    8 eggs
    4 teaspoons butter
       Salt
       White pepper

Preheat oven to 375°. Generously butter custard cups or cups of a muffin tin. Break an egg into each cup, season with salt and pepper, dot with butter, and bake 10 to 12 minutes or until just done. Turn out onto individual serving plates. Serves 8.

ENGLISH STYLE SAUSAGE

    1½ pounds lean pork shoulder
     ½ pound pork fat
     2 tablespoons minced parsley
     2 teaspoons salt
     1 teaspoon sage
     1 teaspoon marjoram
     1 teaspoon brown sugar
     ¼ teaspoon ground red pepper
        (cayenne), optional
     ⅛ teaspoon thyme

Grind the shoulder and pork fat together. Combine with the remaining ingredients in a large bowl, mixing well with hands. To taste for seasoning, make a small patty of the mixture and fry. Add more seasoning to the bowl if necessary. Form balls the size of walnuts and flatten into patties. Fry lightly on both sides until well done but not dry. Serves 6 to 8.

HOT BISCUITS

See Basics, page 183.

SPICED HONEY

    1 cup honey
    ¼ teaspoon ground cloves
    ¼ teaspoon cinnamon

Add the cinnamon and cloves to the honey, mixing thoroughly. Let stand at least 30 minutes before serving.

ENGLISH BREAKFAST TEA

Prepare commercially packaged English breakfast tea according to package directions.

Begin the Day in Style

BROILED GRAPEFRUIT

FLUFFY OMELET

CHIPPED BEEF OR HAM SAUCE

TOASTED CHEESE BREAD

SPICED PEACH PRESERVES

Nothing turns an ordinary day into an extraordinary one faster than a lovingly prepared, delectable breakfast. Here for those special mornings—an anniversary, perhaps, a son or daughter home from college, or just a leisurely Sunday—is a breakfast to remember. You'll never think of grapefruit as diet food again once you've tried it brushed with butter, sugar, and a dash of Angostura bitters, then popped under the broiler. As for the rest of the repast—a sauced omelet, toasted cheese bread, and peach preserves—well, it speaks for itself.

BROILED GRAPEFRUIT

4   grapefruit
Butter
Sugar
Angostura bitters

Cut the grapefruit in half. With scissors or a grapefruit knife, remove pith and membrane in the center. Place in the hollow center of each ¼ teaspoon butter, ¼ teaspoon sugar, and a few dashes bitters. Place on cookie sheets and broil 4 inches from heat about 5 minutes. Serves 8.

FLUFFY OMELET

6   eggs, separated
3   teaspoons flour
2   teaspoons cornstarch
1   cup milk
½   teaspoon salt
Dash pepper
2   tablespoons butter
Chipped Beef or Ham Sauce
(recipe follows)

Preheat oven to 350°. Beat yolks of the eggs with the flour and cornstarch. Add the milk, salt, and pepper. Beat the whites until stiff but not dry and fold carefully and lightly into the yolk mixture.

Melt the butter in a large skillet, preferably nonstick. It must be ovenproof. When the butter begins to sizzle, add the egg mixture. Bake for 20 minutes. When done, loosen edges and slip, right side up, onto a heated serving platter.

Spoon a ribbon of chipped beef or ham sauce over the omelet. Pass the remaining sauce. Serves 6.

CHIPPED BEEF OR HAM SAUCE

2   cups Béchamel Sauce (see Basics, page 170)
1   tablespoon butter
1½ cups chopped chipped beef or ham
1½ teaspoons dry mustard
1   teaspoon Worcestershire sauce
Dash salt, if necessary

Make a béchamel sauce, according to the directions in Basics. Melt the butter in the top of a double boiler over simmering water. Add the meat and sauté, stirring occasionally. Add the béchamel sauce, mustard, and Worcestershire sauce. Taste carefully before adding the salt since these meats can be very salty. Stir and cook until smooth and well blended.

TOASTED CHEESE BREAD

Make cheese bread according to the directions in Basics, page 182. Slice and toast before serving.

SPICED PEACH PRESERVES

1   cup frozen peaches, sweetened or unsweetened, thawed
Juice of ½ lemon
¾   cup sugar, or to taste
½   teaspoon cinnamon
⅛   teaspoon cloves
10 candied cherries, optional
2   tablespoons chopped walnuts, optional

In a heavy saucepan, combine the peaches, lemon juice, sugar, cinnamon, and cloves. Cook slowly until thickened, stirring occasionally. The cherries and walnuts may be added if desired; they are for appearance only. The preserves may be served either hot or cold.

A Connoisseur's Choice

CHAMPAGNE   MACADAMIA NUTS

SWEETBREADS IN CREAM   POPOVERS

STRAWBERRIES CAMILLE

Sweetbreads fall into that unique category of foods—along with such other diverse delicacies as anchovies, fruitcake, sauerkraut and garlic—that seem to attract either ardent admirers or violent detractors. There seems to be no middle ground here. Either you love 'em or you hate 'em—and I definitely love 'em. If you've never prepared sweetbreads before, you'll find that the method that follows is foolproof and the results absolutely divine. And certainly no one will ever again accuse you of serving run-of-the-mill breakfasts!

As for dessert, there is no middle ground when it comes to strawberries. Is there anyone alive whose mouth doesn't begin to water at the mere thought of their luscious, red-ripe sweetness? They are beyond question my favorite berry (a fact well known to my family and friends, who never let my June birthday go by without indulging me in pints and pints of strawberries). If you feel the way I do, you'll have to agree that strawberries Camille is the most sublime, incredible way ever of enjoying this fabulous fruit.

SWEETBREADS IN CREAM

2   pounds sweetbreads
¼   cup lemon juice
1   teaspoon salt

Regardless of the final presentation of the sweetbreads, it is important that the initial preparation always be as follows. Soak the sweetbreads in icewater with 1 teaspoon salt for 1 hour. Drain. Bring 4 cups water and the lemon juice to a boil. Add the sweetbreads and cook, simmering, for 20 minutes. Drain and chill. Carefully remove the membranes with a sharp knife. The sweetbreads are now ready for use in any recipe.

CREAM SAUCE FOR SWEETBREADS

2   tablespoons butter
     Dash salt
     Dash white pepper
2   cups Chicken Stock (see Basics, page 168)
¼   cup dry white wine
½   pound fresh mushrooms
2   tablespoons butter
2   egg yolks
½   cup cream or evaporated milk

Slice the sweetbreads and sauté in 2 tablespoons melted butter, seasoning with salt and white pepper. Heat the chicken stock and pour it over the sweetbreads. Add the wine. Cook, basting constantly, until the sweetbreads are glazed.

Wash and slice the mushrooms. Sauté in the remaining 2 tablespoons butter. Place the sweetbreads and mushrooms in a warmed serving dish, reserving liquid in sweetbread pan. Beat the egg yolks with the cream. Add a little of the sweetbread liquid to the cream mixture and beat well. Now turn all of the cream mixture into the pan and whisk evenly. Heat gently, but do not boil, until thickened. Pour the sauce over the sweetbreads and mushrooms. Cut tops from popovers, fill with sweetbreads and cream and replace the tops, slightly askew. Serve immediately. Serves 8.

POPOVERS

See Basics, page 183.

STRAWBERRIES CAMILLE

Providing at least 6 per serving, wash and dry very large, ripe strawberries, leaving the hulls in place. Arrange the berries on a bonbon tree (available in specialty shops) or pile them in a large bowl or on a round platter. Place this in the center of the table.

Present each guest with a small glass of a sweet dessert wine, such as a sweet Sauterne, and have a small dish of sifted powdered sugar at each place. Each guest takes one berry at a time, dipping it first in the wine and then in the sugar. This, indeed, is food for the gods. Drink the wine, of course.

Luncheons

A Touch of Genius

CITRON PERRIER   CHEESE STRAWS

ARTICHOKES WITH CRABMEAT STUFFING

STRAWBERRY ROLL

Perrier water with a touch of lemon is *not* old-fashioned lemonade. To accompany it, we have cheese straws made from pie pastry, cheese, and a whiff of cayenne. Don't let the simplicity of the stuffed artichoke fool you. It is easily filling enough for the most ravenous guest, and everyone will want to devote his or her complete attention to this delectable entrée. For a dessert nobody will be able to resist, bring on the strawberry roll!

CITRON PERRIER

1 lemon
2 oranges
1 12-ounce can frozen lemonade
Perrier water or other mineral water

Combine the juices of the lemon and oranges with the lemonade concentrate. Dilute with the appropriate amount of water, using half Perrier water. Pour over ice cubes to serve. Serves 6 to 8.

CHEESE STRAWS

1 5-ounce jar sharp cheese
¾ cup flour
1 teaspoon paprika
⅓ cup butter
¼ teaspoon salt
Dash ground red pepper (cayenne)

Preheat oven to 400°. Using a food processor or an electric mixer, or mixing by hand, combine all ingredients well. To make straws, force through a pastry bag or cookie press, using the star tip, onto a greased cookie sheet. Form into long ropes and cut at 3-inch intervals before baking. Bake 8 to 10 minutes, until golden. If desired, sprinkle with paprika. Makes 36 to 48.

ARTICHOKES WITH CRABMEAT STUFFING

6 to 8 artichokes
1½ cups Béchamel Sauce (see Basics, page 170)
1 can crabmeat, drained
½ cup mild cheddar cheese, shredded
3 to 4 tablespoons dry bread crumbs
1 or 2 lemons

Trim and clean artichokes, cutting the points off each leaf. Remove all of the feathery portion of the center, digging and scraping with a sharp spoon. Insert a slice of lemon in the cavity of each artichoke. In one or more large saucepans, bring to a boil enough water to come about two thirds of the way up the artichokes. Drop in the artichokes, adding a little lemon juice or vinegar to the water to prevent them from darkening. They should cook 35 to 45 minutes, depending on size. Test for doneness by inserting a cake tester into the bottom of one of the artichokes. It should be tender. Turn upside down on paper toweling to drain.

Make béchamel sauce according to the directions in Basics. Fold in the crabmeat and taste for seasoning. Preheat oven to 350°.

Fill the cavity of each artichoke with the crabmeat sauce and place them on a cookie sheet. Top each one with some of the shredded cheese and bread crumbs. Heat for 10 minutes and then place under broiler for a few minutes to brown the cheese and crumbs. Serves 6 to 8.

STRAWBERRY ROLL

1 Sponge Cake Roll (see Basics, page 186)
8 ounces cream cheese, softened
3 tablespoons sugar, superfine preferred
3 tablespoons orange-flavored liqueur
1 quart fresh strawberries
Powdered sugar

Prepare and bake the sponge cake roll according to the directions in Basics. Combine the cream cheese, sugar, and liqueur well. Unroll the cake and spread the filling evenly. Slice half of the strawberries and scatter them over the cream cheese filling. Roll the cake and chill.

Crush the remaining strawberries and flavor with additional sugar and liqueur to taste. Pass to spoon over the cake. Just before serving, sprinkle the roll with sifted powdered sugar. Slice on the diagonal for larger-appearing slices. This is a good dessert to slice and serve at the table. Serves 8 to 10.

May Bowle

MAY BOWLE

LEMON CRESS SANDWICHES

CUCUMBER SANDWICHES

CHICKEN SALAD SERENDIPITY

INDIENNE SAUCE   SOUR CREAM SAUCE

MADELEINES   TOASTED ANGEL FOOD

MACAROONS

The May Pole is up
Now give me the cup
I'll drink to the garlands around it
But first unto those
Whose hand did compose
The glory of flowers that crowned it.
A Pleasant Grove of New Fancies (1657)

This punch of strawberries marinated in sugar and brandy and covered with chilled white Moselle wine really could be served any time, but in spring, buy traditional May wine with woodruff. You couldn't find a better accompaniment for the punch than lemon cress sandwiches with the pungency of watercress, and cucumber sandwiches, fluffy with cream cheese and chives. Chicken salad is rescued from the ordinary by its presentation—a colorful garnish of avocado, tomato and olives—and serendipity is achieved when you pass the sour cream sauce and Indienne sauce. Those lining up for dessert will waver between French madeleines, toasted angel food, and macaroons. Have plenty—they'll probably try them all.

MAY BOWLE

1 quart fresh strawberries
1 cup sugar
1 cup brandy
3 bottles May wine or Moselle or
   Rhine wine

Wash and hull the strawberries. Place in a bowl and cover with the sugar and brandy. Chill in refrigerator for at least 3 hours.

Make a decorative ice ring for the May Bowle if you can. Do this by pouring a small amount of water into a ring mold, just enough to cover the bottom by ¼ inch. Wash carefully an assortment of spring flowers such as purple and yellow violets and place on water. Freeze. Fill the mold with water and freeze again.

Place the marinated strawberries in a punch bowl, reserving one berry for each wine glass to be served. Fill the bowl with the chilled white wine and float the ice ring in the center. Serve in stemmed wine glasses with a strawberry in each. Makes 16 servings.

LEMON CRESS SANDWICHES

1 cup butter, softened
  Dash salt
¼ teaspoon sugar
2 to 3 teaspoons lemon juice
1 bunch watercress
1 loaf firm white bread, sliced lengthwise, crusts
  removed

Cream the butter and add salt, sugar, and lemon juice. Remove the stems from the watercress and wash well. Dry the leaves on paper towels and add to the butter mixture. Go over long bread slices with rolling pin to compress. Spread filling evenly on bread. Starting from the short end, roll the sandwiches very tight. Wrap in waxed paper or plastic wrap and chill for at least 1 hour. Just before serving slice very thin, forming pinwheels. Makes 24.

CUCUMBER SANDWICHES

1 cucumber
  Dash salt
3 ounces cream cheese, softened
2 to 3 teaspoons chives, snipped
1 loaf firm white bread

Peel the cucumber, cut in quarters lengthwise, and remove the seeds. Chop fairly fine. Cream the cream cheese and add the salt and chives. Add the cucumber just before you are to serve the sandwiches to avoid having the mixture become too watery. Spread on ovals or rounds of white bread, crusts removed. These are to be served open faced.

For another presentation, spread the filling on long slices of white bread that have been sliced lengthwise, as for lemon cress sandwiches. Cover with another slice of bread. Press slightly to make sandwiches firm, and cut the long sandwiches into 2-inch squares. Makes 36.

CHICKEN SALAD SERENDIPITY

1   whole chicken or capon
1   carrot
1   rib celery
2   sprigs parsley
1   whole medium onion
1   teaspoon salt
    Dash pepper
2   cups celery, chopped
1   cup Mayonnaise (see Basics, page 174)
1   tablespoon lemon juice
    Sour Cream Sauce (see Basics, page 176)
    Indienne Sauce (see Basics, page 176)
    Crisp lettuce leaves
2   tomatoes, cut in wedges
2   avocados, sliced in fingers
1   16-ounce can pitted black olives
1   8-ounce can smoked salted almonds

Bring enough water to boil to cover the chicken. Add the carrot, celery rib, parsley, onion, salt, and pepper. When it returns to the boil, add the chicken and simmer until tender, about 1¼ hours. Remove the chicken from the stock, reserving the stock and straining it for another use. When chicken is just cool enough to handle, remove the meat from the bones, trimming off all skin and fat. Cut the meat into chunks and combine with the chopped celery. Mix the mayonnaise with the lemon juice, and using just enough to moisten the salad well, toss this with the chicken and celery. Taste for seasoning and chill.

To serve, line a large bowl or platter with crisp lettuce. Place the salad in a mound in the center. Garnish lavishly with tomato wedges, avocado fingers, black olives, and smoked salted almonds. The sour cream sauce and Indienne sauce are passed at the table. They are to be used to heighten the flavor of the salad, if desired, in the manner of a dipping sauce. Serves 8 to 10.

MADELEINES

2   eggs
¼   cup sugar
    Dash salt
¼   teaspoon rum or vanilla
¼   cup flour
¼   cup butter, melted and cooled
    Powdered sugar, sifted

Preheat oven to 325°. Grease and flour madeleine shell pans very well.

Combine the eggs and sugar, adding the salt. Beat well until mixture ribbons. Add the rum or vanilla. Sift the flour over the mixture. Fold it in by hand, using a rubber scraper. Work very gently to avoid reducing the volume of the eggs. Now fold in the melted butter gently but thoroughly, checking to be sure that no butter remains at the bottom of the bowl and that all has been incorporated into the batter.

Quickly fill the molds ⅔ full. If individual shell molds are being used, place these on a cookie sheet. Bake 12 to 15 minutes. Watch carefully to prevent overbaking. Unmold immediately onto a rack and sprinkle with sifted powdered sugar. Sprinkle with powdered sugar again after they have cooled. Makes 24.

TOASTED ANGEL FOOD

1   loaf angel food cake, purchased
1   cup fine granulated sugar
    Grated rind of 1 orange
½   cup butter, melted

Cut the cake into the shape of petits fours
(cubes about 2 inches square). Work the
orange rind into the sugar with your fingers,
or use the blender or food processor.

Paint the cake cubes on all sides lightly with
a brush dipped in the melted butter. Roll them
in the flavored sugar and place on ungreased
cookie sheets. Toast lightly under the broiler
just before serving. Watch carefully to prevent
burning. Makes 40.

MACAROONS

½   pound almond paste
1   cup sugar
3   egg whites, unbeaten
    Powdered sugar, sifted

Preheat oven to 300°. Line a cookie sheet
with kitchen parchment paper.

Mix the almond paste and sugar. Work this
very well until it is thoroughly combined and
the almond paste is lightened. Add the egg
whites, one at a time, beating well after each
addition. The mixture will be slightly lumpy.

Spoon the mixture into a pastry bag fitted
with the round tube and form round cookies
on the paper lined cookie sheet. (It is not
essential to use a pastry bag. The cookies can
be dropped from a spoon.) Dipping the tips of
your fingers in water, moisten the tops of the
cookies and sprinkle with sifted powdered
sugar.

Bake about 25 minutes. To remove the
cookies from the paper, gently lift the paper
off the cookie sheet and invert it onto a rack
or board. Using a brush dipped in water, wet
the paper over each cookie, and they will
loosen and fall off. Makes 24.

A Gastronome's Delight

DRY COCKTAIL SHERRY

SKEWERED GRAPES AND SWISS CHEESE

COQUILLES SAINT-JACQUES

CHERRY TOMATO SALAD

MELBA TOAST AUX FINES HERBES

PROFITEROLES AU CARAMEL

Skewered grapes and Swiss cheese are a novel accompaniment for dry sherry. Guaranteed to delight the palate of any gastronome, the familiar and always welcome Coquilles Saint-Jacques is paired with a beautiful cherry tomato salad topped by an interesting sour cream dressing. Melba toast spread with herb butter provides just the right crunchiness. There could be no better ending to a fine luncheon than tiny profiteroles, served London style with a divine caramel sauce.

SKEWERED GRAPES AND SWISS CHEESE

On small wooden picks, alternate green
seedless grapes with cubes of Swiss cheese of
approximately the same size as the grapes.
The skewers are most attractive with either
three or five items on each pick, depending on
the length of the picks. Arrange them on a
large tray and pass with the sherry.

COQUILLES SAINT-JACQUES

1   cup dry white wine
½   cup water
4   black peppercorns
1   teaspoon salt
1   bay leaf
2   pounds scallops, or more
1   pound mushrooms, sliced
2   tablespoons butter
2   cups Mornay Sauce (see Basics, page 170)
    Parmesan cheese, grated
    Buttered bread crumbs

Combine the wine, water, peppercorns, salt,
and bay leaf in an enameled or stainless steel
pan. Bring to a boil, drop in the scallops, and
return to the boil. Reduce heat and simmer
just until the scallops become translucent.
Drain, reserving the broth.

Sauté the mushrooms in the butter, being
careful not to overcook. Toss them lightly
with the scallops. Make the Mornay sauce
according to the directions in Basics.

Butter scallop shells or individual
flameproof serving dishes and pile in the
scallops and mushrooms. Spoon the Mornay
sauce over until covered. Sprinkle with the
Parmesan cheese and bread crumbs. Dot with
butter. Broil about 3 inches from the heat
until bubbly and slightly browned.

If using scallop shells, it is wise to use
paper coasters or similar slip-proof material
to prevent the shells from sliding around on
the plates. Have them small enough so that
they won't be easily seen. Serves 8.

CHERRY TOMATO SALAD

1   quart cherry tomatoes
1   head Boston lettuce
½   cup sour cream
¼   cup Mayonnaise (see Basics, page 174)
1   tablespoon lemon juice
1   tablespoon chopped green onion
½   teaspoon horseradish

Pour boiling water over the cherry tomatoes
and let stand 30 seconds. Drain and peel. Chill.
Separate the leaves of the Boston lettuce and
wash and dry. Combine the remaining
ingredients. Season to taste with salt and
pepper if desired. Just before serving, place a
leaf of lettuce on each plate. Pile the tomatoes
on the lettuce, cutting any large tomatoes in
half. Spoon the dressing over. This salad may
be served on the same plate as the coquilles.
Serves 8.

MELBA TOAST AUX FINES HERBES

1   cup butter
2   tablespoons green onions or chives,
    chopped
2   tablespoons parsley, chopped
1   teaspoon fresh tarragon or basil,
    chopped, or ½ teaspoon, dried
1   loaf French bread, thinly sliced

Preheat oven to 350°. Combine the butter and
herbs. Spread the bread slices with the herb
butter, place on a cookie sheet and toast in
oven until golden. Watch carefully. These
may be made ahead of time and served cold
or reheated briefly in oven.

PROFITEROLES AU CARAMEL

1 recipe Choux Paste (see Basics,
   page 184)
1 recipe Pastry Cream (see Basics,
   page 191)
1 recipe Caramel Sauce (see Basics,
   page 189)

Make walnut-sized puffs according to the directions in Basics. When cool, fill each puff with some of the pastry cream. Cover the bottom of a large, flat serving dish with a thin layer of caramel sauce. Place the puffs in a single layer on top of the sauce. Pour the remaining caramel sauce into a bowl and pass with profiteroles at the table. Serves 8.

A Lesson in Perfection

GREEN BEANS WITH MIMOSA GARNISH

CHICKEN CRÊPES   PEACHES WITH CHUTNEY

LIME ICE WITH BLUEBERRIES

PINOT CHARDONNAY (CALIFORNIA) OR

POUILLY-FUISSÉ (FRENCH)

The advent of the French Nouvelle Cuisine during recent years has created as great a stir among gastronomes as did Carême and Escoffier in their day. To my mind, it is a much welcome—and long overdue—advance. Here is a menu that represents the epitome of "new cooking"—simple and classic in its appeal. As the French chefs Jean and Pierre Troisgros have asked, "Why damage or mask the flavor of fine meat, the verdant freshness of spring vegetables?" This delightful luncheon, featuring a rainbow of colors, taste, and texture, is indeed a lesson in perfection.

GREEN BEANS WITH MIMOSA GARNISH

2   pounds green beans
1   cup Vinaigrette Sauce (see Basics,
    page 173)
2   eggs, hard-cooked
1   tablespoon parsley, chopped

Wash and remove ends of fresh green beans. Bring a large kettle of unsalted water to the boil and drop the beans in, a handful at a time, being careful to keep the water boiling. (Always cook green beans whole. Do not salt the water because it will toughen them.) Boil 8 to 10 minutes, until tender-crisp. To test for tenderness, drop a bean into a cup of cold water to cool, then test by biting into it.

Drain the beans and immediately drop them into a large bowl of ice water. Chilling the beans quickly in this manner will help preserve their beautiful bright color and prevent further cooking. Drain, cover with the vinaigrette sauce, and marinate at room temperature at least 2 hours, tossing occasionally to be sure all the beans are coated.

To make the mimosa garnish, separate the whites from the yolks of the hard-cooked eggs and chop finely. Force the yolks through a sieve and then toss with the chopped parsley.

Pile the beans, all facing the same direction, onto individual salad plates. Spoon a ribbon of yolk across the center of each pile and then a narrow ribbon of chopped whites on either side. Serves 8.

CHICKEN CRÊPES

16 Entrée Crêpes (see Basics, page 185)
2   4-ounce cans sliced mushrooms
3   cups cooked white meat of chicken or
    turkey, coarsely chopped
2   cups Béchamel Sauce (see Basics,
    page 170)
1   cup Swiss cheese, shredded

Preheat oven to 350°. Butter enough rectangular flat baking pans to hold 16 rolled crêpes.

Sauté the mushrooms in the butter, seasoning with salt and white pepper if desired. Combine the mushrooms with the chicken and 1¼ cups béchamel sauce, working gently. Spread a couple of tablespoons of filling down the center of each crêpe and roll. Place in baking pans, seam side down. Cover with foil and heat in oven about 15 to 20 minutes.

Just before serving, spoon a ribbon of the remaining béchamel sauce down the length of the pan of crêpes, sprinkle with the cheese, and place under the broiler until bubbly. Place two crêpes on each serving plate and garnish with peach with chutney. Serves 8.

PEACHES WITH CHUTNEY

8   large peach halves
8   teaspoons chutney, chopped

Select good quality canned peaches. Cut a tiny slice from the rounded side of each half so that it will sit level on the plate. Fill the cavity of each peach with a fine chutney. Serves 8.

LIME ICE WITH BLUEBERRIES

1   pint blueberries
2   tablespoons sugar, superfine preferred
¼   cup orange-flavored liqueur
1   quart lime sherbet, or more

Toss the blueberries gently with the sugar. Pour the liqueur over the berries and marinate in the refrigerator at least 1 hour, stirring occasionally. To serve, place a scoop of lime sherbet in each stemmed glass. Pour a small spoonful of blueberries and some syrup over each serving.

For a more dramatic presentation, place the stemmed glasses of sherbet in the freezer an hour or so before serving time so that they will be frosted when you bring them to the table. Quickly spoon the blueberries over the sherbet after removing from the freezer. Serves 8.

A Fine Lunch for Friends

CREAM OF CELERY SOUP RAMON

BIG SALAD   POPPY SEED BARS

NUTCAKE ROLL WITH BUTTERSCOTCH SAUCE

One of my favorite meals, be it luncheon or supper, is simply soup and salad. Cream of celery soup Ramon is absolutely exquisite. No one would dream that mild-mannered celery could pack such a culinary punch! Big salad is just that—a huge bowl of lettuce tossed with vinaigrette sauce and encircled with dishes of garbanzo beans, salami, and myriad vegetables. Poppy seed bars are such a snap to prepare, you won't believe they could add so much to the meal. Save your fanciest flourish for last: a feather-light nutcake roll, sliced diagonally and served with an ethereal butterscotch sauce.

CREAM OF CELERY SOUP RAMON

1 bunch celery
3 cups Chicken Stock (see Basics, page 168)
1 cup Béchamel Sauce (see Basics, page 170)
2 egg yolks, optional
2 tablespoons heavy cream, optional
½ cup Dry Croutons (see Basics, page 177)

Using a vegetable peeler, remove the strings from the celery. Chop it coarsely and cook in a saucepan with the chicken stock until tender. Drain the celery, reserving the stock. Purée the celery in a blender or food processor or force it through a food mill.

Combine the strained stock, puréed celery, and béchamel sauce. Heat and taste for seasoning. If desired, just before serving combine the egg yolks and cream, blending well. Add a little of the soup to the egg mixture to thin and warm it; then whisk it into the soup. Be very careful not to let the soup come to a boil after the egg yolks have been added, or the eggs will scramble, giving a curdled appearance. Adding egg yolks and cream in this manner is called "enriching" a dish. You will notice that the resulting soup has a much creamier texture and richer appearance and taste. Enriching is not necessary, however, particularly if you are watching calories and cholesterol.

You can follow this recipe exactly, substituting broccoli, asparagus, cauliflower, green peas, carrots, or any other vegetable that strikes your fancy. Sprinkle each serving with a few croutons. Serves 8.

BIG SALAD

1 16-ounce can garbanzo beans (chick peas)
   Vinaigrette Sauce (see Basics, page 173)
3 heads assorted lettuces
½ pound salami, cut in julienne strips
8 green onions, sliced
6 ribs celery, sliced
1 bunch radishes, sliced
1 green pepper, sliced
   Parsley, chopped
   Cherry tomatoes, cut in half

Drain the garbanzo beans. Rinse in cold water, place in a small saucepan, add fresh water, and bring to a boil. Drain and marinate in vinaigrette sauce, unrefrigerated, 2 hours or longer. Wash, dry, and tear lettuce and place in a plastic bag. Chill. Just before serving, toss the greens with vinaigrette sauce. Drain the garbanzo beans and add them to the salad, along with the salami, vegetables, and parsley. Toss lightly and garnish with cherry tomatoes.

This salad may be served buffet style or passed at the table for the guests to help themselves. Serves 8.

POPPY SEED BARS

1 loaf thick-sliced firm white bread
¼ pound butter, melted
   Poppy seeds

Preheat oven to 375°. Remove crusts from bread. Cut each slice into four strips. Using a pastry brush, paint the bread strips lightly with melted butter on one side and dip lightly in poppy seeds. Place on cookie sheets and bake about 8 to 10 minutes, or until brown. May be served either warm or cold.

NUTCAKE ROLL
WITH BUTTERSCOTCH SAUCE

    6 eggs, separated
    ¾ cup sugar
    1 cup walnuts, chopped
       Pinch salt
    1 teaspoon baking powder
       Pinch cream of tartar
    1 cup heavy cream
    2 tablespoons sifted powdered sugar,
       or more
       Butterscotch Sauce (see Basics
       page 189)

Preheat oven to 350°. Grease a 15½x10½x1-inch jelly roll pan and line it with waxed paper. Grease the waxed paper.

Beat the egg yolks until light. Add the sugar gradually, beating until the mixture is very light and lemon colored and forms a ribbon when the beaters are lifted. Remove the beaters and, working by hand, fold in the walnuts, salt, and baking powder. Beat the egg whites with a pinch of cream of tartar until stiff but not dry. Fold into the yolk mixture. Spread the batter evenly in the pan and bake for 15 to 20 minutes, or until it tests done with a cake tester.

Sprinkle the top with powdered sugar; cover with a clean kitchen towel and then a board or heavy flat cardboard. Invert the pan onto the board, thus turning out the cake onto the towel. Carefully peel off the waxed paper. Trim off any crisp edges if necessary. Turn edge of towel over the cake and, beginning with the long side, roll the cake and towel together. Cool on rack.

Whip the cream and sweeten with the powdered sugar to taste. Unroll the cake and spread with the whipped cream. Roll the cake again and sprinkle with sifted powdered sugar. Chill in the refrigerator at least 2 hours. To serve, slice on the diagonal to make larger looking servings. Pass butterscotch sauce at the table. Serves 8 to 10.

Just a Little French

KIR   GOUGÈRES

JAMBON PERSILLE   FRENCH BREAD

STRAWBERRIES WITH CRÈME FRAÎCHE

WHITE BURGUNDY (CALIFORNIA) OR

CABERNET BLANC (FRENCH)

Un petit français, s'il vous plaît. . . . First, offer a specialty of Burgundy: cheesey gougères and kir, a refreshing summer combination of white wine and black currant liqueur. Jambon persille—parsleyed ham—is served cold in a gelatin aspic. *Pour le dessert, des fraises avec crème fraîche*—and if you've never tasted the latter, my version of this French delicacy comes as close to duplicating the unique tartness and texture of real crème fraîche as is possible this side of the Atlantic. *Bon appetit!*

KIR

Into a stemmed wine glass, pour 1 to 1½ ounces Crème de Cassis. Add a couple of ice cubes if desired, and fill the glass with a good dry white wine such as a California mountain white, a German Moselle, or a white Burgundy. The proportion of Crème de Cassis to wine can be varied according to taste.

GOUGERÈS

Choux Paste (see Basics, page 184)
¼ pound Swiss cheese, grated

Preheat oven to 400°. Grease a cookie sheet generously.

Make the choux paste according to the directions in Basics. Reserve about 3 tablespoons of the cheese, and add the remainder to the dough. Using a pastry bag with the round tip, or dropping the paste from a teaspoon, form a crown of walnut-sized puffs on the cookie sheet. Make them close enough together so that they will touch when baked, but do not overcrowd them. Sprinkle each puff with some of the reserved cheese. (Leftover paste may be used to make individual puffs or, if you choose, you may make tiny individual puffs instead of the crown. For tiny puffs, follow the baking directions in Basics.)

Bake 15 minutes at 400°. Reduce the oven temperature to 350° and continue baking 8 to 10 minutes more, or until brown and dry. Serve the crown whole. Guests serve themselves by breaking off a puff at a time. Serves 8.

JAMBON PERSILLE

2 cups Chicken Stock (see Basics, page 168)
1 cup dry white wine
2 bay leaves
6 black peppercorns
3 shallots, chopped
1 clove garlic, minced
1 tablespoon chopped fresh tarragon, or 1 teaspoon dried
1 tablespoon parsley, chopped
1 teaspoon thyme
1 pound canned or boneless ham
2 tablespoons unflavored gelatin
¼ cup cold water
1 tablespoon vinegar
1 cup parsley, chopped

Combine the first nine ingredients. Add the ham and any juices from the ham. Bring to a boil and simmer 20 minutes. Remove the ham from the liquid and dice coarsely. Press into a 1½-quart glass bowl or terrine.

Strain the stock and measure out 3 cups, adding water if necessary to get this quantity. Soak the gelatin in ¼ cup cold water to soften and heat gently until dissolved. Add to the stock. Pour a small amount of the stock over the ham and place in the freezer to set quickly.

Add the vinegar and chopped parsley to the remaining stock. Pour over the ham and refrigerate until set.

Jambon persille may be served unmolded, but traditionally it is cut out of the bowl or terrine. Serve with warm French bread, sweet butter, and of course, Burgundy. Serves 6 to 8.

FRENCH BREAD

See Basics, page 180.

STRAWBERRIES WITH CRÈME FRAÎCHE

1   **quart fresh strawberries**
2   **tablespoons superfine sugar, or more**
2   **tablespoons Kirsch, or more**
    Crème Fraîche (see Basics, page 187)
3   **tablespoons unsalted pistachio nuts, chopped**

Wash, hull, and slice the strawberries from top to bottom in the French manner. Lightly toss them with sugar and Kirsch, adding more flavoring if desired. Marinate in the refrigerator at least 1 hour. Spoon into serving dishes, top with a spoonful of crème fraîche, and sprinkle with pistachios. Serves 8.

Raspberries may be used for this dessert if desired. Follow this recipe, but leave the raspberries whole.

Lunch on the Patio

SKEWERED FRUIT WITH CURRY SAUCE

BASQUE OMELET

HONEY WALNUT BREAD WITH CREAM CHEESE

CHENIN BLANC (CALIFORNIA) OR

VOUVRAY (FRENCH)

We Minnesotans cling to pleasant memories of spring and summer to help us survive the never-ending frosty months of winter. One of the warmest and fondest of these images is of lunch on the patio, that sun-kissed day in May or June when it is at last possible to dine *al fresco*. For such a long-awaited occasion, nothing could be more welcome than skewers of fresh fruit dipped in curry sauce, followed by a Spanish-inspired omelet glistening with nuggets of tomato, ham, green pepper, and onion. Thin slices of honey walnut bread spread with cream cheese complete a glorious meal.

SKEWERED FRUIT

Select a variety of fresh fruits in season, such as melon balls, strawberries, and pineapple chunks. Do not use soft fruits such as oranges, pears, or peaches. Arrange, alternating, on 7-inch wooden skewers. Place the skewers on a large platter so that the guests may help themselves. Have a dish of curry sauce nearby for the guests to spoon on their plate.

CURRY SAUCE

1   tablespoon butter
1   teaspoon curry powder
¾   cup juice from sweet pickles
     Vinegar, if needed
     Sugar, if needed
2   tablespoons arrowroot or cornstarch
2   tablespoons cold water

Melt the butter in a small pan. Add the curry powder and sauté, stirring for 1 minute. Add the sweet pickle juice, adding more vinegar and sugar if needed to heighten the flavor. Boil 4 minutes to combine flavors. Dissolve the arrowroot or cornstarch in the cold water and add to the sauce. Cook, stirring constantly, until thickened and clear. This sauce may be served either warm or cold, but cannot be rewarmed because the cornstarch will break down and the sauce will become thin again.

BASQUE OMELET

2   tablespoons oil
2   green peppers, chopped
1   medium onion, chopped
1   clove garlic, minced
3   tomatoes, peeled, seeded, and
     coarsely chopped
¼   pound ham, chopped, optional
     Salt
     Pepper
     Sugar
     Basil
1   tablespoon butter
2   eggs per serving, slightly beaten
1   teaspoon water per serving
     Chopped parsley
     Fried bread

In a large skillet, sauté the peppers and onion in oil until the onion is soft and transparent, but not brown. Add the garlic and tomatoes, and ham if desired. Simmer about 20 minutes. Season with salt, pepper, sugar, and a pinch of basil; simmer until the flavors have blended. Taste for seasoning and adjust if necessary.

For each serving, lightly beat the eggs, water, and a dash of salt with a fork until they are just mixed. Heat an omelet pan or a nonstick skillet until a drop of water will dance. Drop in the butter and swirl around the pan with a fork to grease the entire surface. When the butter is sizzling, but before it begins to turn brown, add the eggs. As they cook on the bottom, pull them toward the center of the pan from the sides with a fork, letting the uncooked eggs roll to the sides, turning and tilting the pan as necessary. When the egg mixture has lost its gloss, but is not quite set on the top turn out onto the plate, folding the second half of the omelet over the first half as it slips out of the pan. Spoon some of the vegetables around the omelet, top with some chopped parsley, and scatter some diamonds of fried bread around the edges. Serves 6 to 8.

To make the fried bread, remove crusts from slices of firm white sandwich bread. Butter on both sides and fry until golden brown in an ungreased skillet. Cut into diamond shapes. These can be made ahead and reheated in a 350° oven.

HONEY WALNUT BREAD WITH CREAM CHEESE

1 cup milk
1 cup honey
½ cup sugar
¼ cup soft butter
2 egg yolks
2½ cups flour, sifted
1 teaspoon salt
1 teaspoon baking soda
½ cup chopped walnuts
8 ounces cream cheese, softened
Dash salt
1 teaspoon sugar, preferably superfine
1 teaspoon Kirsch or any orange-flavored liqueur, optional

Preheat oven to 325°. Grease and flour a 4x8-inch loaf pan.

Scald the milk. Add the honey and sugar and stir until the sugar is dissolved. Cool. Beat in the butter and yolks. Combine the flour, salt, and soda. Sift. Add to the honey mixture, blending well. Stir in walnuts. Pour into the prepared pan and bake about 45 minutes or until it tests done with a cake tester. Remove from pan and cool on a rack. Serve thinly sliced with sweet butter or flavored cream cheese.

To make the flavored cream cheese, combine the last four ingredients.

Suddenly
It's Spring!

SOUP BONNE FEMME

SPRING SALAD

FRENCH CHOCOLATE CAKE

According to an old fisherman's axiom, "The first day of spring is one thing, and the first spring day is another. The difference between them is sometimes as great as a month." When, one fresh and beautiful morning, you awaken to discover that the first spring day has at last made its appearance, greet it proudly with this wonderful luncheon. Begin with a soup that's pure gold: leeks, onion, and potatoes, simmered in chicken broth. Move on to a salad chockful of every fresh vegetable you can imagine—radishes and beans and peas and whatever else you can lay your hands on. Finally, astound your guests with the richest chocolate cake they've ever tasted, a celestial French *gâteau.*

SOUP BONNE FEMME

4 leeks or 8 green onions
1 small onion
4 tablespoons butter
4 cups Chicken Stock (see Basics,
   page 168)
   Salt
   Pepper
4 medium potatoes, peeled
2 cups hot milk

Cut the root ends off the leeks and separate to wash thoroughly. Examine carefully to see that all the dirt is removed since leeks tend to conceal soil between the leaves. Use all of the white portion and part of the green. Mince. Dice the onion finely and sauté the leeks and onion in 2 tablespoons of the butter until soft. Cover and cook over low heat 10 to 15 minutes until very soft and transparent. Add the chicken stock, salt, and pepper. Dice the potatoes, soak in cold water for a few minutes, drain, and add to the soup. Simmer, uncovered, for about 40 minutes.

Just before serving, add the hot milk and the remaining 2 tablespoons of butter. Do not let the soup come to a boil after the milk has been added. Taste for seasoning. Pour into a heated tureen. Serves 6 to 8.

This recipe makes a fine vichyssoise if you wish to serve a cold soup. After simmering, force the soup through a food mill if possible, or blend it in the blender or food processor. Chill well and add heavy cream to taste. Sprinkle with snipped chives before serving.

SPRING SALAD

1 bunch radishes, sliced
1 cup cooked green beans, cut
1 cup cooked green peas
1 15-ounce can artichoke hearts,
   packed in water
1 cucumber, seeded and diced
1 cup Vinaigrette Sauce (see Basics,
   page 173)
3 hard-cooked eggs
12 cherry tomatoes, halved, or more
1 head iceberg lettuce, shredded
2 tablespoons parsley, chopped
   Russian Dressing (see Basics, page 175)

In a salad bowl place your choice of the vegetables listed above, all or any number of them. You may, of course, substitute vegetables in season as you wish. Marinate them in vinaigrette sauce for at least 30 minutes.

Just before serving, drain off the excess vinaigrette. Add the shredded lettuce to the bowl and toss lightly. Garnish with the eggs cut in wedges and the cherry tomatoes. Mask with a few spoonfuls of Russian dressing. Sprinkle the top with chopped parsley. Pass remaining Russian dressing. Serves 6 to 8.

FRENCH CHOCOLATE CAKE

½   cup butter
⅔   cup sugar
3   eggs, separated
4   1-ounce squares semisweet chocolate
½   teaspoon almond extract
¾   cup cake flour, sifted
    Pinch of salt
¼   teaspoon cream of tartar
2   tablespoons sugar
    Chocolate Whipped Cream Frosting
    (recipe follows)

Note: Because there is no leavening other than cream of tartar in this cake, its lightness depends on careful incorporation of the beaten egg whites into the batter. The texture will be quite different from that of American cakes—denser, creamier, and richer.

Preheat oven to 350°. Grease and flour an 8-inch round cake pan. Melt the chocolate in the top of a double boiler over simmering water and cool slightly.

Cream the butter with the ⅔ cup sugar until light and fluffy. Add the egg yolks and beat well. Add chocolate to the butter mixture. Fold the almond extract and cake flour into the batter. Beat the egg whites with the salt and cream of tartar until stiff but not dry, adding the remaining 2 tablespoons of sugar gradually and beating until the sugar is dissolved. Gently fold the whites into the batter. Pour the batter into the prepared pan and bake about 25 minutes or until the cake is puffed and the center does not move when the pan is shaken slightly.

Cool in the pan on a rack 10 minutes and then carefully remove the cake to a rack to cool completely. Fill a pastry bag with the frosting and pipe it around the outside edge of the top of the cake. Sprinkle the center with sifted powdered sugar.

CHOCOLATE WHIPPED CREAM FROSTING

1   cup whipping cream
¼   cup cocoa, preferably Dutch process
½   cup powdered sugar, sifted
    Dash salt

Combine and mix well all ingredients. Chill at least 2 hours or overnight in the refrigerator. Whip just before using.

Magnifique

AVOCADO MAGNIFIQUE

CHEESE SOUFFLÉ

ORANGES ORIENTAL   GINGER COOKIES

PINOT CHARDONNAY (CALIFORNIA) OR

MÂCON BLANC (FRENCH)

The French have a word for it. . . magnifique. One might never think of filling avocado halves with such unlikely ingredients as orange juice, vinegar, walnuts, and tomato paste and then broiling them, but one taste and you'll become a believer. Your palate will be more accustomed to the tangy cheese soufflé that follows, but no less gratified. Such a meal could end only with a dish as exotic as oranges oriental—deceptively simple to prepare, but what intrigue for the taste buds! Serve a spicy ginger cookie on the side and listen to your guests murmur "ooh la la!"

AVOCADO MAGNIFIQUE

4 avocados, not too ripe
2 sprigs parsley
1 rib celery
1 green onion
1 clove garlic
⅓ cup white wine vinegar
1 teaspoon salt
¼ cup orange juice
  Half 6-ounce can tomato paste
1 tablespoon brown sugar
¼ cup walnuts or pecans
1 teaspoon dry mustard
  Dash pepper
1 cup oil

Place parsley, celery, green onion, garlic, vinegar, and salt in a blender or food processor. Let stand 10 minutes in order for the salt to dissolve; then blend just until the vegetables are minced. Add the orange juice, tomato paste, brown sugar, and nuts and process again to combine. Add the mustard and pepper. If using a blender, add the oil in three parts, blending a few seconds after each addition. If using a food processor, add the oil slowly, processing constantly. Taste for seasoning.

Peel the avocados and cut them in half lengthwise. Fill the center of each with dressing. Just before serving, broil about 4 minutes. Serves 8.

CHEESE SOUFFLÉ

1 tablespoon Parmesan cheese, grated
3 tablespoons butter
3 tablespoons flour
1¼ cups milk
4 eggs, separated
  Dash ground red pepper (cayenne)
  Dash nutmeg
¾ cup Swiss cheese, grated
½ teaspoon salt

Preheat oven to 350°. Butter a 1½-quart soufflé dish and sprinkle with the Parmesan cheese.

Melt the 3 tablespoons butter in a heavy-bottomed saucepan. When the butter begins to bubble, add the flour all at once and cook, stirring constantly, for 2 minutes. Add the milk and cook, stirring, until thickened and smooth. Beat the yolks together and add a small amount of the milk mixture to warm and thin the eggs. Then add the yolks to the sauce and stir thoroughly to blend, Add the salt, red pepper, nutmeg, and then the cheese. Cool.

Beat the whites of the eggs until stiff but not dry and fold into the cheese mixture. Pour into the prepared soufflé dish. Run the handle of a wooden spoon around the top, 2 inches from the edge. This will produce the classic "crown" as the soufflé bakes. Bake about 35 minutes. Serve immediately. Serves 4. For more servings, make two soufflés rather than doubling the size.

ORANGES ORIENTAL

6 oranges
1 cup sugar
½ cup water
  Half 10-ounce jar red currant jelly
  Dash Cointreau

With a vegetable peeler, peel the oranges very thinly, making sure that none of the white membrane is included in the strips of peel. Cut the peel into tiny julienne strips. Put in a small saucepan and cover with cold water. Bring to a boil and continue boiling for 5 minutes. Drain and repeat this process. Drain again. Remove all the white membrane from the fruit of the oranges. Slice into a glass compote and sprinkle with Cointreau.

Make a syrup by boiling together the sugar, ½ cup water, and currant jelly until the sugar and jelly are dissolved. Drain, reserving syrup. Add the peel strips to the syrup and cook 5 minutes. Pour the syrup with the peel over the oranges and chill for at least 2 hours. Serves 6 to 8.

GINGER COOKIES

1   cup sugar
¾   cup shortening
1   egg
¼   cup molasses
½   teaspoon salt
2   cups flour, sifted
2   teaspoons baking soda
1   teaspoon cinnamon
1   teaspoon ginger
½   teaspoon cloves

Preheat oven to 350°. Grease cookie sheets.

Cream the sugar and shortening until light and fluffy. Add the egg and beat well. Add the molasses and salt and beat well. Combine the dry ingredients and add to the mixture. Chill 1 hour. Form into small balls, about the size of a melon ball, and roll in granulated sugar. Bake about 15 minutes, or until done. Makes about 5 dozen.

Epicure's Choice

VEGETABLE COCKTAIL

QUENELLES WITH SEAFOOD SAUCE

ICE CREAM AND MANDARINS WITH

BAKED MERINGUE TOPPING

CHABLIS (CALIFORNIA OR FRENCH)

It would be difficult to find a more elegant, truly epicurean luncheon menu than this. Students in my French cooking classes often balk at the prospect of making quenelles. "Are they really worth the effort?" they ask. The answer, once they have tasted the fruits of their labors, is always a resounding yes. Today, of course, one can use a food processor to turn out these little morsels of gastronomical delight. Begin your luncheon with a simple yet impressive vegetable cocktail: shredded lettuce and vegetable gems coated with vinaigrette, then layered in a wine glass and drizzled with Russian dressing. For an unusual, but most fitting, finale, feature a surprisingly tasty combination of ice cream, mandarin oranges, and meringue.

VEGETABLE COCKTAIL

1½ cups shredded lettuce
1½ cups tiny flowerettes cauliflower
¾ cup carrots, shredded
¾ cup zucchini, sliced and cut in wedges
     but not peeled
¾ cup celery, cut finely on bias
1 tomato, chopped and slightly drained
     Vinaigrette Sauce (see Basics, page 173)
     Russian Dressing (see Basics, page 175)
     Fresh tarragon or parsley

Using a stemmed wineglass for each serving, layer the vegetables in the glass as follows. Place a little shredded lettuce in the bottom, drizzle with a touch of viniagrette. Add a layer of cauliflower, more lettuce, and a little vinaigrette. Now add a layer of grated carrots, some lettuce and a little vinaigrette. Add a layer of zucchini, lettuce, and vinaigrette. Top with a layer of celery and a layer of tomato. Place a generous dollop of Russian dressing on the top of the cocktail and decorate with a sprig of fresh tarragon or parsley. Remember to keep each of the layers very thin so as to avoid making the salad too large. Serves 6 to 8.

QUENELLES

1 pound filet of sole or halibut
1 teaspoon salt
½ teaspoon white pepper
¼ teaspoon nutmeg
2 egg whites, unbeaten
1 cup evaporated milk
     Seafood Sauce (recipe follows)
     Dry bread crumbs

Force the fish through a meat grinder twice, or process in a food processor, turning on and off rapidly, until a smooth purée is formed. Put the fish in a blender or leave in the food processor bowl. Blend, adding the seasonings and egg whites. Pour into a bowl set over a larger pan or bowl filled with ice cubes. Working with a rubber scraper, work in the evaporated milk until it is thoroughly incorporated.

Form the quenelles with two spoons dipped in hot water, using one to spoon the mixture out of the bowl and the other to smooth the top. Carefully push the quenelles from the spoon into a large shallow pan of salted simmering water. Be careful not to overcrowd the pan. Poach, uncovered, 15 minutes. It is important that the poaching water is not allowed to boil. Remove from the water with a slotted spoon and arrange in a buttered shallow baking dish. Reserve until half an hour before serving.

Preheat oven to 350°. Heat quenelles for 10 to 15 minutes in the oven. Remove from oven, cover with hot Seafood Sauce, sprinkle with bread crumbs, and slip under the broiler just until browned. Serves 6 to 8.

SEAFOOD SAUCE

2 tablespoons butter
1 tablespoon sweet Hungarian paprika
2 tablespoons flour
2 cups evaporated milk or half-and-half
½ teaspoon salt
     Dash white pepper
1 pound mushrooms, sliced
2 tablespoons butter
½ pound cooked shrimp, coarsely cut
¼ cup brandy

Melt the first 2 tablespoons butter in a heavy saucepan. Add the paprika and cook, stirring, for 1 minute. Add the flour and cook until bubbling. Add the evaporated milk or cream all at once and cook, stirring constantly, until thickened. Do not let boil. Season to taste with salt and pepper.

In a skillet, sauté the mushrooms in the remaining 2 tablespoons butter until just tender crisp. Add, together with the shrimp, to the sauce.

In a small saucepan, warm the brandy. Carefully light it with a long match or a candle and pour it, flaming, into the sauce. Stir to blend.

ICE CREAM AND MANDARINS WITH BAKED MERINGUE TOPPING

1   quart vanilla ice cream
1   16-ounce can Mandarin orange sections
4   tablespoons orange-flavored liqueur
4   egg whites
½   cup sugar
     Dash salt
     Powdered sugar

Make small balls of the ice cream, place on cookie sheet, and return to freezer. Drain Mandarin orange sections and marinate for at least 1 hour in 2 tablespoons of the orange-flavored liqueur.

Alternate layers of ice cream balls and oranges in a soufflé dish. Drizzle the marinating liquid from the oranges over the ice cream. Return to the freezer until just before serving.

Preheat oven to 425°. Make a meringue by beating the egg whites until stiff but not dry, gradually adding the sugar and salt after soft peaks have formed. Flavor with the remaining 2 tablespoons of liqueur. Spread the meringue over the ice cream, covering completely, and sprinkle with powdered sugar.

Fill a pan with chopped ice. Place the soufflé dish in the bed of ice and bake about 5 minutes. Serve immediately. Serves 6 to 8.

Eating In or Out of Doors

CHILLED WHITE WINE

SALTED ALMONDS   OLIVES

SALMAGUNDI

PÂTÉ MAISON MEYER   FRENCH BREAD

COFFEE ÉCLAIRS

"Salmagundi," the dictionary tells us, is a word of obscure origins meaning "hodgepodge." Whatever it means, I find it both a delightful word and a delightful way of capturing the essence of summer's bounty. Begin with the freshest homegrown vegetables you can find, cook them *al dente* and marinate while warm in a tangy vinaigrette sauce. Chill them thoroughly, then arrange with raw vegetables on a large platter or in individual *raviers*. Salmagundi may be large or small, bland or pungent, plain or fancy, but it must be cool, neat, and ravishing to both eye and palate. As an accompaniment, there is nothing finer than your own pâté, served with slices of warm French bread and chilled white wine of your choice. Top off the meal with coffee éclairs and your guests will go home truly sated.

SALMAGUNDI

Prepare the items listed below. (See Basics, page 173, for Vinaigrette Sauce.) Place them in *raviers* (matching oblong serving dishes) if possible, and line them up on the buffet table.

Pickled Mushrooms: Combine in a saucepan 2 tablespoons lemon juice, 1 tablespoon chopped onion, 3 tablespoons olive oil, ¼ teaspoon salt, and a pinch of thyme. Add 1 pound fresh mushrooms, thinly sliced, or 8 ounces canned button mushrooms. Simmer until the fresh mushrooms are just tender crisp, about 3 to 4 minutes. If using canned mushrooms, simmer 5 minutes to blend the flavors. Cool in the juice. Drain to serve.

Marinated Celery: Peel ½ bunch celery with a vegetable peeler to remove the strings. Cut in 2- to 3-inch lengths, halving the wider pieces vertically. Cook in beef stock just until fork tender, about 8 minutes. Drain cooking liquid, cover with vinaigrette sauce while the celery is still hot, and chill. Arrange in rows in a serving dish and top with Mustard Vinaigrette (see Basics, page 173).

Cucumbers with Sour Cream Sauce: Peel 2 cucumbers, leaving on a little of the green. Run the tines of a fork lengthwise down the cucumbers to score the edges. Cut in half lengthwise, and remove the seeds with a sharp spoon. Slice, not too thinly, and arrange in a serving dish. Top with Sour Cream Sauce (see Basics, page 176).

Tomatoes Vinaigrette: Drop 2 or 3 tomatoes into a pan of boiling water for 10 seconds. Remove and peel. Slice in the French manner from top to bottom, rather than horizontally. Place in serving dish in overlapping rows and sprinkle with chopped fresh basil, if available, or dried basil. Drizzle with vinaigrette sauce.

Pickled Beets: In a saucepan place a 1-pound can tiny whole beets or sliced beets, with their juice, ¼ cup vinegar, ¼ cup sugar, 8 whole cloves, 1 stick cinnamon, ¼ teaspoon salt, and, if desired, a dash of Angostura bitters. Simmer 4 minutes and allow to cool in the juice. Drain to serve.

Marinated Carrots: Peel ½ pound carrots and slice thinly on the oblique. Cook in boiling salted water until just tender crisp, about 6 minutes. Drain and cover with vinaigrette sauce. Chill. Sprinkle with chopped parsley to serve.

Buttered Radishes: Clean radishes thoroughly and cut off the tops and stems. Make a tiny hollow in the top of each radish and fill with butter. Arrange, tops up, in the serving dish.

Tuna in Aïoli Sauce: Thoroughly drain one 7-ounce can white albacore tuna. Spread ½ cup Aïoli Sauce (see Basics, page 175) in the bottom of a serving dish. Invert the can of tuna, gently easing it from the can so as to retain the shape as much as possible. Place a dollop of sauce on top and garnish with a little pimiento and a mixture of chopped fresh chives and parsley.

PÂTÉ MAISON MEYER

½ pound side pork, thinly sliced
2 eggs
2 shallots, finely diced
1 onion, grated
2 teaspoons salt
1 teaspoon parsley, chopped
1 teaspoon marjoram
½ teaspoon thyme
½ teaspoon pepper
⅛ teaspoon allspice
⅛ teaspoon cloves
⅛ teaspoon nutmeg
3 pounds ground pork
½ pound chicken livers
2 bay leaves

Preheat oven to 375°. Line a 2-quart pâté mold or loaf pan with the strips of side pork, reserving enough to cover the top of the pâté. In a large bowl, place the eggs and beat lightly. Add the shallots, onion, and all of the spices except the bay leaves. Add the ground pork and mix well with hands. Cook the chicken livers in a small amount of chicken stock or water until almost done. Drain them, then chop and add to the meat mixture. At this point you may check for seasoning by pressing about 1 tablespoon of the mixture into a small patty and frying it.

Press the mixture into the mold, being sure to fit it into the corners and patting down well to condense and flatten it. Cover with reserved side pork and place the bay leaves on top. Cover, using foil if a lid is not available. Place in a larger pan and add hot water to about halfway up the mold. Bake for 2 hours.

Remove cover. Place foil directly on top of the pâté and weight with something heavy, like a brick or canned foods. Cool and chill, weighted, overnight. Turn out of mold and scrape off the side pork. Slice thinly and serve with French bread. Serves 6 to 8.

FRENCH BREAD

See Basics, page 180.

COFFEE ÉCLAIRS

Choux Paste (see Basics, page 184)
Pastry Cream (see Basics, page 191)
Mocha Frosting (see Basics, page 191)
1 teaspoon instant expresso coffee

Preheat oven to 425°.

Make the choux paste according to the directions in Basics. Force through a pastry bag fitted with the round tip onto a greased baking sheet, making each éclair about 3 inches long. Bake in the lower part of the oven for 15 minutes; then reduce heat to 350° and bake 10 to 15 minutes longer. Cut a hole in the side of each éclair to allow steam to escape while cooling.

Dissolve the instant coffee in 1 tablespoon boiling water. Cool and add to the pastry cream. Cut the éclairs in half lengthwise and fill with the flavored pastry cream.

Make the mocha frosting; frost the éclairs. Makes 14.

Lunch in the Garden Court

CREAM OF WATERCRESS SOUP   TOASTIES

GARDEN COURT SEAFOOD SALAD

BRANDIED PEACHES WITH ICE CREAM

RIESLING (CALIFORNIA) OR MOSELLE (GERMAN)

One of the most beautiful American restaurants I remember, the Garden Court in San Francisco's Palace Hotel, is the inspiration for this elegant meal. If there is a better menu for a ladies' luncheon, I have yet to see it. Begin with a subtle cream of watercress soup accompanied by whimsical toasties—artful little constructions of white bread shapes. Next comes the incomparable Garden Court salad: a medley of seafood, shredded lettuce, and tomato drizzled with vinaigrette and Russian dressing. Finally, present a chilled peach half poached in wine, capped with a tiny scoop of ice cream, and topped with a luscious liqueur-spiked sauce.

CREAM OF WATERCRESS SOUP

2   bunches watercress, heavy stems
    discarded
3   cups Chicken Stock (see Basics,
    page 168)
1   cup Béchamel Sauce (see Basics,
    page 170)
2   egg yolks, optional
2   tablespoons heavy cream, optional

Coarsely chop all but half a bunch of the watercress. Add to the chicken stock and cook until tender. Drain, reserving the stock. Purée the watercress in a blender or food processor or force it through a food mill.

Combine the strained stock, the puréed watercress and the béchamel sauce. Taste for seasoning, adding salt and white pepper if necessary. If desired, just before serving, combine the egg yolks and cream, blending well. Add a little of the soup to the egg mixture to thin and warm it; then whisk this mixture into the soup. Be very careful not to let the soup come to a boil after the egg yolks have been added, or they will scramble, giving a curdled appearance. Finely chop the remaining half a bunch of watercress and add to the soup just before serving. Serves 6 to 8.

TOASTIES

20 slices firm white bread
¼   cup butter, melted

Preheat oven to 350°. Using a donut cutter, cut rounds from 16 slices of bread. Remove the crusts from the remaining 4 slices of bread and cut them in half. Cut each half into 6 narrow strips. Paint all the pieces with the melted butter. Place 3 strips into the hollow center of each round. Place on a greased cookie sheet and toast in the oven for about 8 minutes or until golden brown. Makes 16.

GARDEN COURT SEAFOOD SALAD

1   head lettuce
¼   cup Vinaigrette Sauce (see Basics,
    page 173)
8   slices tomato
3   pounds cooked seafood: cod, shrimp,
    lobster, or crabmeat in any combination
2   cups Russian dressing (see Basics,
    page 175)
3   hard-cooked eggs
3   to 4 sprigs parsley, chopped
    Celery root or artichoke hearts for
    garnish, optional

Shred lettuce and make a nest of it on each plate. Drizzle with vinaigrette sauce. Place a slice of tomato on top. Make a seafood salad by mixing your choice of seafood with 1 cup Russian dressing. Mound salad on top of each tomato slice. Remove yolks from hard-cooked eggs and force through a sieve. Chop the whites finely. Toss the yolks and whites lightly with the parsley. Arrange this mimosa garnish in a ring at the base of each salad. Garnish if desired. Pass remaining Russian dressing. Serves 8.

BRANDIED PEACHES WITH ICE CREAM

8   canned peach halves with syrup
¼   cup sugar
¼   cup dry white wine
¼   cup Marsala
3   tablespoons red currant jelly
2   tablespoons Cointreau or apricot brandy
8   small vanilla ice cream balls

Drain peaches and reserve. Place the syrup in a saucepan and add the sugar, white wine, Marsala, and currant jelly. Cook until the sugar and jelly are dissolved. Add the peach halves and poach over medium heat about 8 minutes. Cool peaches in syrup; then drain, place in dessert dishes, and chill. Bring the syrup back to a boil and cook briskly until reduced in volume by half. Cool and chill. At serving time, add Cointreau or apricot brandy to the syrup. Fill the center of each peach half with an ice cream ball and top with the syrup. Pass extra syrup. Serves 8.

Let's Borrow from the French

ALSATIAN WINE   STUFFED CELERY SLICES

QUICHE LORRAINE

SUNBURST FRUIT SALAD

Let's borrow from the French. How many times do we do just that when we are looking for the ultimate in chic, sumptuous dining? Here the main attraction is quiche Lorraine, a dish whose popularity has taken off in the United States in recent years. Unfortunately, the soggy pastry passed off as quiche by so many American restauranteurs bears no resemblance to the classic creation found in the province whose name it bears. Certainly no French housewife would dare to serve such a tired, bland combination of custard and pie crust, baked or microwaved to lukewarm lifelessness. If quiche is to be the *pièce de résistance* of your menu, as it is here, it must be worthy of the honor: fresh, rich, and silken, studded with bits of crisp bacon and melted Emmenthaler or Gruyère, set off by flaky pastry and baked to a turn. When preceded by stuffed celery slices and followed by a luscious fruit salad, there is no finer luncheon dish.

STUFFED CELERY SLICES

8   ounces cream cheese, softened
3   ounces blue cheese, softened
⅓   cup chives, snipped
2   tablespoons dry sherry
    Dash Worcestershire sauce
1   bunch celery

Combine all ingredients except celery in a mixer or food processor, or by hand. Place in a pastry bag fitted with a ½ inch round tip.

Remove any imperfect outer stalks from the celery. Trim the tops. Loosen the stalks, but do not separate them from the base; rinse thoroughly under cold, running water to remove all soil. Pat dry with paper toweling. Pipe cheese filling into each stalk, re-forming the bunch as the stalks are filled. Wrap the celery in plastic wrap and chill for several hours. Slice into 1-inch slices to serve. An alternate method is to cut off the base of the celery and fill each stalk; then re-form the bunch as nearly as possible, tie, and wrap.

QUICHE LORRAINE

½   recipe Pie Pastry for Hors d'Oeuvres
    (See Basics, page 185)
¼   pound Emmenthaler or Gruyère, sliced
¼   pound bacon, cooked
4   eggs
1   cup evaporated milk or half-and-half
1   tablespoon flour
¼   teaspoon salt
    Dash ground red pepper (cayenne)
    Dash nutmeg

Make pastry according to the directions in Basics and fit into a quiche pan or pie plate. Preheat oven to 375°.

Forming a spiral, alternate slices of cheese and strips of bacon around the bottom of the pie shell. Beat the eggs until blended and add the remaining ingredients. Strain and pour over the cheese and bacon. Bake about 40 minutes or until a cake tester comes out clean when inserted in the center of the quiche. Serves 6 to 8.

SUNBURST FRUIT SALAD

Shredded lettuce
Melon balls
Pineapple chunks
Seedless green grapes
Apple wedges
Avocado fingers
Honey French Dressing (see Basics,
page 174)

Make a bed of lettuce on individual salad plates. Arrange the apple wedges and avocado fingers in a sunburst pattern on the lettuce and scatter the melon balls, pineapple chunks, and grapes over all. Drizzle with honey French dressing.

Dinners

Let's Have Fish Tonight

CRUDITÉS WITH GREEN GODDESS DRESSING

FISH FILETS IN BROWN BUTTER

POTATOES ROSTI

LEMON ICE CREAM   LACE COOKIES

MOUNTAIN WHITE (CALIFORNIA) OR

VOUVRAY (FRENCH)

We Minnesotans, though landlocked in the middle of North America, are more fortunate than many Americans when it comes to the availability of fresh fish. Our more than ten-thousand lakes produce a netfull of freshwater species, most notable among them northern pike and walleye. "Let's have fish tonight" is indeed a welcome invitation, especially when the main course is graced with such side dishes as potatoes rosti—a Swiss version of hash browns—and raw vegetables with your own homemade green goddess dressing. After such a repast, your guests will be lucky even to have room for some refreshing lemon ice cream with lace cookies!

CRUDITÉS

Select a variety of raw vegetables, such as carrots, celery, green pepper, radishes, cauliflower, and zucchini. Wash the vegetables and cut into sticks or slices or flowerettes as appropriate. Arrange in groups on a large serving platter. Serve with Green Goddess Dressing (see Basics, page 176), well chilled.

FISH FILETS IN BROWN BUTTER

¼ cup butter
8 fish filets
  Salt
  Pepper
½ teaspoon thyme
1 large onion, sliced
  Paprika
2 tablespoons parsley, chopped

Preheat the oven to 350°. Cut up the butter and scatter the pieces in a large, flat baking pan. Put the pan in the oven and, watching it carefully, allow the butter to brown but not burn. Remove the pan and lay the fish filets in the butter, turning once to coat both sides. Season with salt, pepper, and thyme. Place the onion slices on top of the filets. Return to the oven and bake about 15 minutes or until the fish flakes. Discard the onion and place the fish briefly under the broiler to brown. Sprinkle with paprika and parsley before serving. Serves 8.

POTATOES ROSTI

6 to 8 baking potatoes
½ teaspoon salt
2 tablespoons oil
2 tablespoons butter

Cook the potatoes in boiling water to cover 10 to 15 minutes, depending on size. They should be cooked but still quite firm. Drain and cool. Peel, cover with plastic wrap, and refrigerate at least 1 hour. Shred with a coarse grater or food processor fitted with shredding disc. Toss lightly with the salt. Heat the oil in a large skillet, preferably nonstick. Add the butter and melt. Press the potatoes evenly into the pan. Cook over medium heat until golden brown on the bottom and heated through. Invert on a heated platter to serve. Serves 6 to 8.

LEMON ICE CREAM

6 tablespoons lemon juice
3 tablespoons lemon rind, grated
2 cups sugar
¼ teaspoon salt
2 13-ounce cans evaporated milk

Combine all ingredients in mixing bowl. Pour into freezer trays and freeze until firm, about 2 to 4 hours. Serves 6 to 8.

LACE COOKIES

1¼ cups oatmeal
1 egg
½ cup sugar
2 teaspoons butter, melted
1 teaspoon baking powder
½ teaspoon salt
1 teaspoon vanilla

Preheat oven to 350°. Spread the oatmeal on a cookie sheet and toast in the oven for about 8 minutes. Watch carefully to avoid scorching. Beat the eggs, adding the sugar gradually. Add the melted butter and then the oatmeal and the remaining ingredients. Raise the oven temperature to 400°. Drop dough by the teaspoonful onto greased cookie sheets, keeping far apart. Press down with a spoon. Bake for 4½ to 5 minutes, or until edges turn medium brown. Remove from the cookie sheets onto a rack immediately. Makes 2 dozen.

The Word Is Posh

CONSOMMÉ WITH QUENELLES

BREAST OF TURKEY RAMON

BRUSSELS SPROUTS VERONIQUE

FRENCH ROLLS

PERSIMMONS VERNA

GREY RIESLING (CALIFORNIA)

OR SOAVE (ITALIAN)

"Posh" is one of those marvelously evocative words—like "crunch" or "whisper"—whose very sound conveys its meaning. Originally a British slang term, "posh" is now more widely used to describe anything that is the height of elegance, luxury, or fashion. Yet few people realize that the word is in fact an acronym: it derives from the expression "Port out, starboard home," referring to the favored cabin locations of wealthy first-class passengers aboard transatlantic ocean liners. In any case, here is a dinner menu worthy of any Mrs. Astor ever enjoyed on the Cunard line. Impress your guests with a first course of consommé with quenelles—they needn't worry about a storm at sea spilling the soup. Move on to breast of turkey Ramon, fit for a gourmet but blessedly inexpensive, with Brussels sprouts as a taste and color accent. And, if you have not yet encountered a persimmon, the dessert will provide a truly memorable introduction.

CONSOMMÉ WITH QUENELLES

- 2 quarts Chicken-flavored Consommé (see Basics, page 168)
- ½ pound skinned and boned chicken breasts
- ½ teaspoon salt
- ⅛ teaspoon nutmeg
- ⅛ teaspoon white pepper
- 2 egg whites, unbeaten
- 1 cup evaporated milk

Force the chicken meat through a meat grinder twice or process in a food processor, turning on and off rapidly, until a smooth purée is formed. Place the chicken in a blender or leave in the food processor bowl. Blend, adding the seasonings and egg whites. Pour into a bowl set into a larger pan or bowl of ice cubes. Using a rubber scraper, work in the evaporated milk until it is thoroughly incorporated.

Form the quenelles with 2 small spoons dipped in hot water, using one to spoon the mixture out of the bowl and the other to smooth the top. Carefully push the quenelles from the spoon into a large shallow pan of salted simmering water. Be careful not to overcrowd the pan. Poach, uncovered, 15 minutes, turning once.

Heat the consommé to serving temperature. Fill the soup bowls and carefully drop 3 quenelles into each bowl. Serves 6 to 8.

BREAST OF TURKEY RAMON

- 1 6-pound frozen turkey breast or 4 whole chicken breasts
- ½ cup flour
  Salt
  White pepper
- 1 egg, beaten with 1 teaspoon water
- 1 cup grated Parmesan cheese
- 1 cup dry bread crumbs
- 2 tablespoons oil
- ½ cup Chicken Stock (see Basics, page 168)
- ½ cup dry white wine, or more
- 8 small slices Mozzarella cheese, optional

Partially thaw the turkey breast in refrigerator. Remove skin and membrane. Slice ¼ inch thick. If using chicken breasts, skin and bone the breast, cut in half, and pound with a mallet between two sheets of waxed paper into thin, uniform pieces. Season the flour with salt and pepper and dredge the turkey pieces in it, brushing them so that only a thin coating of flour clings to them. Dip them in the egg and water mixture. Combine the Parmesan cheese and bread crumbs and dip the turkey pieces in this mixture, being careful to produce an even coating. Let rest on a rack at least 30 minutes.

Heat the oil in a heavy skillet, preferably nonstick, and sauté the turkey pieces until they are golden. Remove to a shallow casserole and add the chicken stock and white wine.

Preheat oven to 350°. Bake the turkey pieces for 15 to 20 minutes, until they feel firm when touched with a finger. Remove from oven, and place a slice of Mozzarella cheese on each piece, if desired. Sprinkle with Parmesan cheese and slip under the broiler until the cheese is melted and browned. Serves 8.

BRUSSELS SPROUTS VERONIQUE

2 pounds Brussels sprouts
1 cup Chicken Stock (see Basics,
   page 168)
1 cup Béchamel Sauce (see Basics,
   page 170)
1 cup green seedless grapes
2 tablespoons filberts, toasted,
   skinned and chopped

Prepare filberts by toasting in a 375° oven for 8 to 10 minutes. Rub briskly in a rough cloth to remove the dry skins and chop coarsely.

Wash the Brussels sprouts carefully, removing the discolored outer leaves and trimming the stems. With a sharp knifepoint, make a small *X* in the base of each stem to speed the cooking of this dense part of the vegetable. Cook in the chicken stock until *al dente*, about 12 to 15 minutes.

Butter a shallow casserole and add the sprouts. Combine the grapes with the béchamel sauce and pour over the sprouts. Sprinkle the chopped filberts over the top and brown briefly under the broiler. Serves 8.

FRENCH ROLLS

See Basics, page 181.

PERSIMMONS VERNA

8 persimmons, very soft
  Kahlua or Crème de Cacao
1 cup whipping cream
1 tablespoon powdered sugar
2 tablespoons pistachio nuts, chopped

It is important that the persimmons be ripe. Not until they reach a very soft stage do they become sweet and pleasant to the taste.

Stand each persimmon on its base and cut with a sharp knife down through the top nearly to the base several times, opening the fruit into petals. With your fingers, gently ease them open. Drizzle a small amount of liqueur over each serving.

Whip the cream, sweeten with the powdered sugar, and add a little of the liqueur to flavor. At serving time, spoon some whipped cream into the center of each fruit and sprinkle some chopped pistachios on top. Serves 8.

Some of
My Specialties

RATATOUILLE   FRENCH BREAD

LONDON BROIL

SAUCE OF THE WINE MERCHANT

BUTTERED GREEN BEANS

ÎLE FLOTTANTE

GAMAY BEAUJOLAIS (CALIFORNIA)

OR BEAUJOLAIS VILLAGES (FRENCH)

August would be perfect for this dinner, because all the vegetables that make ratatouille exciting are fresh in your garden or at the market. Though it is served here with London broil, you'll find yourself using sauce of the wine merchant over and over, with filet or steak or even hamburgers. You may remember floating island as an old-fashioned dessert, but you've never tasted this version, with light-as-a-cloud meringue floating on a golden sea of custard. The meringue sparkles with a net of praline.

RATATOUILLE

¼ cup olive oil
1 large onion
1 eggplant, peeled
2 or 3 zucchini, unpeeled
1 green pepper
2 tomatoes, peeled and squeezed
2 cloves garlic, minced
   Pinch each basil, oregano, and summer savory or 1 teaspoon Herbes de Provence (see Basics, page 177)
1 teaspoon salt
½ teaspoon pepper

Chop all the vegetables into ¾-inch pieces. Sauté the onion in some of the olive oil in a large skillet until soft and transparent, but not brown. Remove to a 6-quart saucepan or Dutch oven. Add more olive oil to the skillet and sauté the eggplant until it just begins to turn golden. Add to the onions. Adding more olive oil to the skillet, sauté the zucchini and then the green pepper, adding them to the vegetables in the saucepan. Now add the tomatoes, garlic and seasonings. Cover and cook over low heat for 1 hour. Taste for seasoning. Can be served hot or cold with French bread. as a first course. Serves 6 to 8.

FRENCH BREAD

See Basics, page 180.

LONDON BROIL

1 recipe Marinade for Beef (see Basics, page 178)
3 pounds flank steak, scored
1 tablespoon oil
8 slices firm white bread
   Butter
   Sauce of the Wine Merchant
   (see Basics, page 171)
   Chopped parsley

Prepare the marinade according to the directions in Basics and pour over the steak in a glass dish. Marinate, covered, 3 to 8 hours in the refrigerator, turning occasionally. Bring to room temperature before cooking. Remove the steak from the marinade, pat dry with paper toweling, and brush with oil. Grill over hot coals or under broiler 5 to 7 minutes on each side, or until medium rare.

Cut the bread slices in 3-inch rounds and butter both sides. Fry until golden brown. Place 1 crouton on each plate. Slice the steak on the diagonal as thinly as possible and pile the thin, pink slices on the croutons. Mask with sauce of the wine merchant and sprinkle with chopped parsley. Pass the remaining sauce. Serves 6 to 8.

BUTTERED GREEN BEANS

2 pounds fresh green beans
¼ cup butter
½ teaspoon summer savory
½ teaspoon salt
   Dash pepper

Wash beans and snap off ends. In a large kettle bring 4 to 6 quarts of water to a rolling boil. *Note:* It is important not to salt the water in which the beans are initially cooked, as this will toughen them. Add the beans, return to a boil, and cook for 8 to 10 minutes until the beans are tender but still crunchy, or *al dente*. Be very careful not to overcook. Drain beans and immediately plunge into ice water to halt the cooking and retain the brilliant green color.

Just before serving, melt the butter in a large skillet and add the drained beans, summer savory, salt, and pepper. Toss gently in the butter until heated through.
Serves 6 to 8.

ÎLE FLOTTANTE

Crème Anglaise (see Basics, page 191)
8 **tablespoons Praline Powder**
 (see Basics, page 187)
4 **egg whites**
½ **cup sugar**

Make the crème Anglaise according to the directions in Basics. Cool and chill. Preheat oven to 275°. Butter a 6-cup mold and sprinkle with 2 tablespoons of the praline powder.

Beat the egg whites until stiff but not dry, adding the sugar gradually and continuing to beat until it is dissolved. (You can test for this by rubbing a small amount between your thumb and forefinger to see if you can still feel the granules of sugar.) Fold in the remaining 6 tablespoons of praline powder. Pour the meringue into the prepared mold. Place the mold in a pan of hot water and bake about 25 minutes, or until firm. Cool 5 to 10 minutes, and unmold onto a shallow round dish. Surround with crème Anglaise.

A Meal to Remember

CELERY VICTOR

PORK TENDERLOIN WITH FORCEMEAT STUFFING

SWEET AND SOUR RED CABBAGE

APPLE TATIN

GEWÜRZTRAMINER (CALIFORNIA OR GERMAN)

This is a modern menu—a three-course meal which includes everything you need for color, texture, flavor, and nutrition. Celery Victor, served as a first course, is marinated in vinaigrette sauce and garnished with a rainbow of vegetables. Pork tenderloin with forcemeat stuffing is a tasty and unusual entrée, complimented in every way by the beautiful and tangy red cabbage. And perhaps most memorable of all is the apple tatin, a classic French tart with a golden carmelized top.

CELERY VICTOR

- 6 to 8 ribs celery
- 2 cups Beef Stock (see Basics, page 168)
- 1 cup Vinaigrette Sauce (see Basics, page 173)
- 2 cups shredded lettuce
- 1 cup cucumber, partially peeled and seeded
- 1 tablespoon chopped pimiento
- 2 tomatoes, peeled
- 2 tablespoons chopped fresh parsley

Using a vegetable peeler, remove the strings from the celery. Cut in 3-inch lengths. Cook in beef stock until just fork tender, 4 to 6 minutes. Drain and, while the celery is still hot, pour the vinaigrette sauce over it and chill. When ready to serve as a first course, drain, reserving dressing, and arrange on a bed of shredded lettuce on individual chilled salad plates. Slice the cucumber thinly, cut the tomatoes in wedges, and arrange them on the plates with the celery. Drizzle with a little of the vinaigrette sauce in which the celery was marinated and sprinkle with the chopped fresh parsley. Scatter the pimiento over the celery. Serves 6 to 8.

PORK TENDERLOIN WITH FORCEMEAT STUFFING

- 2 ¾- to 1-pound pork tenderloins
- ¾ pound ground veal
- ¾ pound ground pork
- ¼ cup grated onion
- 2 teaspoons Herbes de Provence (see Basics, page 177)
- 2 teaspoons salt
- ½ teaspoon pepper
- 1 teaspoon marjoram
- 1 teaspoon thyme
- 2 slices firm white bread
- ¼ cup Chicken Stock (see Basics, page 168)
  Salt
  Pepper

Preheat oven to 350°. Split the pork tenderloins nearly in half lengthwise and open like a book. This is called butterflying the meat. Pound it lightly between 2 sheets waxed paper.

To make the dressing, combine the veal, pork, onion, herbes de Provence, salt, pepper, marjoram, and thyme in a bowl. Tear the bread in small pieces and soak it in the stock until saturated. Add to the dressing and mix well.

Spread the stuffing on one of the tenderloins. Top with the second tenderloin and roll up from the long side. Tie the roll with kitchen string every 2 inches or so to hold it together. Season with salt and pepper and place on a rack in a pan with a small amount of water in the bottom. This will prevent the drippings from scorching.

Bake for 1½ to 2 hours, or until a meat thermometer reads 185°. When the meat is done, allow it to rest for 10 minutes before slicing. This will aid in retaining the juices inside the meat and make slicing easier. Arrange the slices on a heated platter to serve. Serves 6 to 8.

SWEET AND SOUR RED CABBAGE

1   head red cabbage
½   onion, sliced
2   tablespoons butter
2   red apples, unpeeled
1   teaspoon salt
½   cup dry red wine
¼   cup red wine vinegar
¼   cup brown sugar

Preheat the oven to 350°. Remove core and shred the cabbage. Soak in cold water for at least 30 minutes. In a heavy casserole sauté the onion in the butter until soft and transparent, but not brown. Drain the cabbage well and add to the onion. Cover the pan and simmer on top of the stove for 20 minutes, until the cabbage is soft. Slice the unpeeled apples and add them to the casserole, along with the remaining ingredients. Bake, covered, in the oven for about 1 hour. Serves 6 to 8.

APPLE TATIN

8   firm apples, such as Golden Delicious
¼   cup butter
½   cup sugar
1   recipe Pie Pastry (see Basics, page 185)
2   cups sugar
2   cups Crème Chantilly (see Basics, page 187)

Preheat oven to 350°. Peel the apples and cut them into thin wedges. Lay them on a buttered jelly roll pan; dot with butter and sprinkle with the ½-cup sugar. Bake until the apples are transparent, about 20 to 30 minutes, stirring occasionally.

Make the pastry according to the directions in Basics and roll into two rounds a little larger than a 9-inch round straight-sided cake pan. Preheat oven to 400°.

Make a caramel by melting the 2 cups sugar in a heavy pan over medium heat until it turns a golden brown. Be careful not to allow it to get too dark. Pour the syrup into two 9-inch round cake pans, reserving some of it for later use. Arrange the apples over the caramel in a spiral pattern. Top with the pastry rounds, allowing them to hang down over the edge of the pan.

Bake the tatins for 15 minutes; then reduce the heat to 350° and bake for 15 minutes longer. Immediately invert the tatins onto two serving plates. Carefully warm the remaining caramel to bring it back to the syrup state and pour it over the top of the tatins. Serve warm or at room temperature. Pass crème Chantilly. Serves 8 to 10.

Top of the Carlin

CUCUMBER RING

POACHED SALMON   CAPERED MUSTARD SAUCE

PARSLEYED NEW POTATOES

BEET SALAD WITH FILBERTS

CRÊPES WITH CHERRY PRESERVES

RHINE WINE (CALIFORNIA)

OR POUILLY FUMÉ (FRENCH)

One of the most delightful dining experiences I have ever enjoyed was a dinner I shared with my grandson at the top of Seattle's Carlin Hotel. Looking down on the lights of the harbor, we savored regional specialties rivaled only by the maritime grandeur of the scenery below. The taste of that meal remains alive in my memory, and so I have tried to reproduce for our mutual pleasure many of the items on the menu that night.

The hallmark of the cooking of the Pacific Northwest seems to be its freshness. Cook the food simply, letting the natural flavors predominate. The crowning glory of this meal is salmon, surely the *sine qua non* of Seattle cuisine. It is complemented by a bevy of vegetables: a cool cucumber ring; new potatoes, steamed in their jackets and dotted with parsley butter; and beet salad dressed with a surprise of filberts. Crêpes with another regional specialty, cherry preserves, will make this a dinner to remember for you, too.

CUCUMBER RING

    3 cucumbers
    1 tablespoon lemon juice
    1 teaspoon Worcestershire sauce
    1 teaspoon salt
    ¼ teaspoon white pepper
    ¼ cup Mayonnaise (see Basics, page 174)
    1 envelope unflavored gelatin
    2 tablespoons cold water
    1 tablespoon hot water
    ½ cup heavy cream
       Green food coloring, if desired
       Small bunch watercress, if available
    ½ cup Vinaigrette Sauce (see Basics, page 173)
  1½ cups mayonnaise
    2 tablespoons chives, chopped
    2 tablespoons parsley, chopped

Peel 2 of the cucumbers, cut in half lengthwise, and scoop out the seeds. Blanch for 5 minutes in boiling water to which the lemon juice has been added. Drain and place in blender or food processor. Process for about 7 seconds. Remove to a bowl and cool. Add the Worcestershire sauce, salt, pepper and ¼ cup mayonnaise. Soak the gelatin in cold water until softened. Add the hot water and stir until completely dissolved. Add to the cucumber mixture. Whip the cream and fold in. Add the food coloring if desired. Oil a 4-cup ring mold and fill with the mixture. Chill at least 3 hours until firm.

Score the unpeeled cucumber lengthwise with the tines of a fork and cut into thin slices. Marinate at least ½ hour in the vinaigrette sauce. Unmold the cucumber ring onto a serving platter and garnish with the watercress and cucumber slices. Stir the chives and parsley into the 1½ cups mayonnaise, and pass with the cucumber ring. Serves 6 to 8.

POACHED SALMON

    4 pounds salmon, whole or steaks
    1 teaspoon salt
       Dash pepper
       Dash thyme
    7 or 8 shallots, chopped
    1 cup white wine
    1 cup clam juice

Season the fish inside and out with the salt, pepper, and thyme. Lay on a double layer of cheesecloth, leaving the ends long enough to use for lifting the fish. Scatter the chopped shallots in the bottom of any nonaluminum pan in which the fish will fit. Add the wine and clam juice and bring to a boil. Lower the fish into the poaching liquid, cover and poach at a simmer until the fish flakes. Carefully lift the fish out of the pan. Skin if desired. Serve at once on a heated platter with Capered Mustard Sauce (recipe follows), or chill the fish and serve with Mayonnaise Verte (see Basics, page 175). Serves 6 to 8.

CAPERED MUSTARD SAUCE

  1½ cups Mustard Mayonnaise (see Basics, page 175)
    1 tablespoon parsley, chopped
    1 tablespoon capers, chopped

Heat mustard mayonnaise gently in the top of a double boiler. Be very careful not to overheat or the sauce will curdle. Stir in the parsley and capers and pass with the fish.

PARSLEYED NEW POTATOES

   24 small new potatoes
    ½ cup butter
    ½ cup parsley, chopped

Wash the potatoes well. Cook in a steamer until barely tender, about 20 to 30 minutes. Remove the skins. Melt the butter in a heavy skillet and shake the potatoes gently in the butter until coated. Sprinkle with parsley. Serves 6 to 8.

BEET SALAD WITH FILBERTS

1   cup filberts, toasted,
       skinned and chopped
1   head lettuce, shredded
½   cup Vinaigrette Sauce (see Basics,
       page 173)
2   cups pickled beets, chopped (see
       "Eating in or Out of Doors," page 58)
1   cup sour cream
       Grated rind of 1 orange
2   tablespoons sugar
¼   cup parsley, chopped

Prepare filberts by toasting in a 375° oven for 8 to 10 minutes. Rub briskly in a rough cloth to remove the dry skins and chop coarsely.

Place a bed of shredded lettuce on each salad plate. Drizzle with a little vinaigrette sauce. Make a mound of pickled beets in the center. Sprinkle with the filberts. Combine the sour cream, orange rind, and sugar. Place a dollop on each salad. Sprinkle with parsley. Serves 6 to 8.

CRÊPES WITH CHERRY PRESERVES

24   Dessert Crêpes (see Basics, page 185)
 1   10-ounce jar cherry jam or preserves
 2   tablespoons Kirsch
       Pastry Cream (see Basics, page 191)
½   cup macaroon crumbs
       Brandy, optional

Fry the crêpes according to the directions in Basics. Combine the jam or preserves and the Kirsch. Spread on the crêpes and roll. Place in a buttered baking pan. Spoon the pastry cream in a wide ribbon down the row of crêpes. Sprinkle with macaroon crumbs. Preheat oven to 350°. Bake the crêpes for 10 minutes. Serve immediately. To flame, heat a little brandy, light, and pour over crêpes. Present with pride. Serves 8.

Suprêmes de Volaille

PEAS AND PEAPODS AUX FINES HERBES

SUPRÊMES DE VOLAILLE   RICE PILAF

SAUTÉED CHERRY TOMATOES

SAVARIN

PINOT CHARDONNAY (CALIFORNIA OR FRENCH)

To open this dinner cook peas French style; then add peapods, parsley, and chives and whisk them to the table while still crisp. Boneless chicken breasts served in a savory sauce with the always welcome rice pilaf will meet with any guest's approval. Then surprise everyone with cherry tomatoes sautéed in garlic-flavored oil. Savarin just has to be one of the world's premier desserts, not as well known as it deserves, but once tasted, never forgotten!

PEAS AND PEAPODS AUX FINE HERBES

½ pound fresh peapods
1 10-ounce package frozen peas, thawed
2 tablespoons butter
1 teaspoon salt
1 teaspoon fresh parsley, chopped
¼ teaspoon dried chervil
¼ teaspoon dried tarragon
½ teaspoon chives, chopped

Snap ends off peapods and remove strings.
Melt the butter in a large skillet. Add the
peas, cover lightly with either a lid or,
preferably, a large lettuce leaf, and cook over
low heat for 4 to 5 minutes until just done.
Discard the lettuce leaf; add the peapods and
seasonings. Stir gently and cook, uncovered,
another minute or two until the peapods are
heated through but still crisp. Serve on
individual warmed plates. Serves 6 to 8.

SUPRÊMES DE VOLAILLE

4 whole chicken breasts
½ cup flour
½ teaspoon salt
¼ teaspoon white pepper
¼ teaspoon paprika
2 tablespoons oil
¼ cup brandy
½ cup Chicken Stock (see Basics,
   page 168)
1 cup dry white wine
½ cup cream or evaporated milk
16 mushroom caps
2 tablespoons butter
1 or 2 tablespoons Beurre Manié
   (see Basics, page 171)

Skin and bone the chicken breasts and cut
them in halves. Place them between 2 sheets
of waxed paper and pound to flatten.
Combine the flour, salt, pepper, and paprika.
Dredge the breasts lightly; then brush to

remove excess flour. Let rest for at least 30
minutes before cooking. Heat the oil in a
skillet and lightly sauté the breasts. Add the
brandy to the pan and carefully ignite with a
match. When it burns down, add the chicken
stock and wine. Cover and simmer over low
heat about 20 minutes.

Meanwhile, slice the mushrooms and sauté
in butter.

When the chicken breasts are done, remove
them to a heated platter and keep warm.
Increase the heat under the skillet and boil the
sauce rapidly, scraping up any bits sticking to
the bottom of the pan. Reduce the heat and
carefully add the cream. Do not bring to a
boil. Thicken if necessary with beurre manié.
Add the sautéed mushrooms and pour over
the chicken breasts to serve. Pass any extra
sauce. Serves 8.

RICE PILAF

See Basics, page 179.

SAUTÉED CHERRY TOMATOES

1 pound cherry tomatoes
1 tablespoon salt
2 tablespoons oil
1 clove garlic, peeled

Wash tomatoes and remove stems. Sprinkle
with the salt and allow to stand for at least 30
minutes. Wipe the salt off with your hands.
Pour the oil in a heavy skillet and rub the
clove of garlic around the pan. Discard garlic.
Heat and add the tomatoes. Shake the pan,
rolling the tomatoes in the oil and heating
them through, but do not actually cook them.
Serve immediately. Serves 6 to 8.

SAVARIN

1   package dry yeast
¼   cup warm water (105 to 115°)
2   eggs
1½ cups flour, sifted
¼   cup warm milk
¼   pound butter, softened
1   teaspoon salt
2   tablespoons sugar
1   cup Simple Syrup (see Basics, page 188)
1   tablespoon Kirsch
¼   cup Apricot Glaze (see Basics, page 188)
2   tablespoons chopped pistachios or
    candied violets
    Crème Chantilly (see Basics, page 187)

Dissolve the yeast in the warm water, adding a few grains of sugar. Beat the eggs and add the flour and warm milk. Stir in the yeast mixture. Work with a wooden spoon until the dough becomes elastic. Cover and let rise in a warm place until double, about 1½ hours.

Cut the butter into 8 to 10 small pieces and add one at a time to the dough, working it in with a slapping motion with a rubber scraper. Be sure that all the butter is incorporated into the dough. Add the salt and remaining sugar and mix well. Generously grease a savarin or Bundt pan or a 6-cup ring mold, and fill with the dough. Cover with a towel and let rise until double.

Preheat oven to 425°. Bake the savarin about 15 minutes, until browned. Remove from mold at once and prick with a toothpick. Return to baking pan. Add the Kirsch to the hot simple syrup and spoon the syrup over the hot savarin, a little at a time, until the cake has absorbed all the syrup. Let cool, then turn out on serving plate and brush with the apricot glaze. Sprinkle the chopped pistachios or candied violets around the top. Serve with crème Chantilly. Serves 6 to 8.

Haute Cuisine

PÂTÉ DE FOIS GRAS   MELBA TOAST

BLANQUETTE DE VEAU   GREEN NOODLES

FRENCH BREAD

CHOCOLATE SOUFFLÉ   CRÈME CHANTILLY

GREY RIESLING (CALIFORNIA)

OR MÂCON BLANC (FRENCH)

Here is a posh dinner, equally appreciated by visiting notables or friends who are knowledgeable about fine food. Blanquette of veal, ringed by fresh mushrooms and tiny carrots, and veiled with velouté sauce, is truly a sublimity of stew. Best of all, it can be prepared a day ahead and reheated with no loss of flavor. Accompaniments add color, texture, and contrast to your menu. And who doesn't have a weak spot for a steaming, fragrant chocolate soufflé? Provide plenty of crème Chantilly and you will have concluded your dinner in style.

PÂTÉ DE FOIS GRAS

Purchase a good brand of imported pâté de fois gras. Chill at least 2 hours. Remove from can intact and slice thinly. Serve with melba toast.

MELBA TOAST

24   slices firm, thin-sliced white bread
½   pound butter, softened

Preheat oven to 300°. Spread the slices of bread with the softened butter. Cut diagonally into triangles. Place on cookie sheets and bake 30 minutes until dry and golden. Makes 48.

BLANQUETTE DE VEAU

3   pounds lean veal cubes
1   quart Chicken Stock (see Basics, page 168)
1   onion studded with 4 cloves
1   teaspoon salt
¼   teaspoon pepper
¼   teaspoon thyme
12   to 16 fresh mushrooms
½   teaspoon salt
1   teaspoon lemon juice
½   pound carrots
2   cups Velouté Sauce (see Basics, page 170)

Cover veal with cold water, bring quickly to a boil, and cook 5 minutes. Drain the veal and rinse all the scum away from both meat and pan. Return to the pan and cover with chicken stock or cold water. Add the clove-studded onion, salt, pepper, and thyme. Bring to a boil, reduce heat and simmer, covered, 1½ hours.

Meanwhile, wash the mushrooms and cook them for 10 minutes in 1 cup water with the salt and lemon juice. Peel carrots and cut into ¾-inch coins. Drop in boiling salted water to cover and cook 10 minutes. Drain.

Remove veal from the pan and reserve, keeping warm. Bring the cooking liquid to a rapid boil and cook until reduced in volume by one-half. Strain. Make velouté sauce, using the reduced cooking juices from the veal for the liquid in the sauce. Supplement with chicken stock if necessary. Add the mushrooms and carrots to the sauce.

Place the veal cubes in the center of a heated serving platter and pour the sauce over the meat. Surround with the cooked green noodles which have been tossed in butter and Parmesan cheese. Serves 6 to 8.

GREEN NOODLES

    Spinach Noodles (see Basics, page 184) or
1   8-ounce package green noodles
1   teaspoon salt
1   teaspoon oil
¼   cup butter, softened
½   cup grated Parmesan cheese

Cook the noodles in boiling salted water, adding the oil to the water to prevent the noodles from sticking together. When the noodles are cooked *al dente*, drain them and toss with the butter and Parmesan cheese.

FRENCH BREAD

See Basics, page 180.

CHOCOLATE SOUFFLÉ

3 tablespoons butter
3 tablespoons flour
¼ teaspoon salt
1 cup hot milk
4 egg yolks
½ cup sugar
3 squares unsweetened chocolate
5 egg whites
   Powdered sugar
   Crème Chantilly (see Basics, page 187)

Preheat oven to 375°. Butter a 1½-quart soufflé dish and fit a buttered parchment paper or aluminum foil collar around the dish. Sprinkle the inside with sugar.

Melt the butter and add flour and salt. Cook and stir until smooth. Add the hot milk and cook until very thick, stirring constantly with a whisk. Beat the yolks and pour a small amount of the sauce over them and quickly blend together. Then add the egg yolk mixture to the sauce in the pan. Stir in the sugar. Melt the chocolate in a small pan over warm water. When melted and smooth, add to the sauce. Cool.

Beat the egg whites until stiff but not dry. Add a small amount of whites to the sauce to lighten it. Now fold the sauce into the remaining egg whites quickly but lightly. Do not work this mixture too much since the egg whites will break down and the soufflé will not be as high and fluffy.

Pour the soufflé into the prepared dish. Bake about 40 minutes. When done, remove the collar and sprinkle the top with sifted powdered sugar. Serve immediately. Pass crème Chantilly. (Instruct your guests to place their whipped cream on the side of the plate; if they put it directly on the hot soufflé, it will break down.) Serves 8.

A Dinner
of Distinction

CONSOMMÉ ROYALE   CURRY TOAST

ROCK CORNISH HENS   ALA WITH NOODLES

PEAS WITH WATER CHESTNUTS

PEARS WITH GRENADINE

BAGUETTES FLAMAND

GAMAY BEAUJOLAIS (CALIFORNIA)

OR SAINT-EMILION (FRENCH)

Rock Cornish hens, raised in this country primarily in Connecticut and New York, are finding their way onto an increasing number of Americans' tables after years of regional specialty status. The small birds make an appealing change of pace from chicken and turkey, and their unique flavor is accented beautifully here by crunchy bulgur wheat with noodles and peas with water chestnuts. Flatter your guests by offering them a truly majestic first course—consommé royale with curry toast rolls. The finale, pears poached in a grenadine syrup, adds the light sweet touch needed for perfect balance and satisfied palates.

CONSOMMÉ ROYALE

2 quarts Beef-flavored Consommé
   (see Basics, page 168)
2 whole eggs
2 egg yolks
   Dash salt
   Dash white pepper
1 tablespoon parsley, chopped, or
1 teaspoon curry powder

Preheat oven to 325°. To make the royale, beat the eggs and yolks. Add ½ cup of the consommé, salt, pepper, and either parsley or curry powder. Mix well. Generously butter a 10x6½-inch pan or another pan of equivalent area. Fill with the custard. Set baking pan in a larger pan of hot water and bake 15 to 20 minutes, or until a knife inserted halfway to center comes out clean. Cut into 1½-inch cubes or, if you have tiny cutters, into fancy shapes.

Heat the consommé. Place a few cubes of royale in each serving cup and fill with the hot consommé. Serves 6 to 8.

CURRY TOAST

16 slices firm white thin-sliced bread
¼   pound butter, melted
½   teaspoon curry, or more if desired

Remove crusts from bread slices. Combine butter and curry powder, and brush lightly on bread. Roll each slice tightly and secure with a wooden pick. Place in jelly roll pan and paint rolls with remaining butter. Bake in 350° oven about 8 minutes just before serving.

ROCK CORNISH HENS

8 Cornish hens
2 tablespoons butter
2 tablespoons oil
1 carrot, roughly chopped
1 rib celery, roughly chopped
1 onion, roughly chopped
2 cups Chicken Stock (see Basics,
   page 168)
1 cup dry white wine
   Salt
   Pepper

Preheat oven to 350°. In a heavy skillet, brown the birds on all sides in the butter and oil. Scatter the vegetables in the bottom of a large roaster with a lid. Place the birds on top of the vegetables. Add the stock and wine. Cover and bake about 1 hour. Remove from oven and season with salt and pepper. Increase oven heat to 450° and return pan, uncovered, to oven briefly to brown the birds. Then remove them to a heated platter and keep warm.

Strain the cooking juices into a saucepan and boil hard over high heat to reduce and intensify the flavor. If desired, you may thicken the juices with a little beurre manié (see Basics, page 171). Pass the sauce with the birds. Serves 8.

ALA WITH NOODLES

3 tablespoons oil
1 small onion, minced
2 cups ala (bulgur wheat)
1 quart Chicken Stock (see Basics, page 168)
1 clove garlic, peeled
1 stick cinnamon
8 whole cloves
1 blade star anise, optional
2 tablespoons butter
1 3-ounce can crisp Chinese noodles

Preheat oven to 350°. Sauté the onion in the oil in a heavy ovenproof casserole until transparent but not brown. Add the ala and stir to coat with oil. Cover with the stock. Add the garlic, skewered on a toothpick, and the spices. Cover and bake about 25 minutes. Remove cover and take out the garlic and spices. Toss with 2 forks to expel steam. Just before serving, add the butter and half the noodles. Toss to incorporate. Sprinkle the remaining noodles on the top. Serves 6 to 8.

PEAS WITH WATER CHESTNUTS

1 5-ounce can water chestnuts, sliced
1 cup Chicken Stock (see Basics, page 168)
2 10-ounce packages frozen green peas, partially thawed
   Salt
1 tablespoon cornstarch dissolved in
2 tablespoons water
   Parsley, chopped

Cook water chestnuts in the chicken stock, covered, for 6 minutes. Add the peas, cover, and cook an additional 6 minutes. Add salt to taste. Stir in the cornstarch and water mixture. Heat, stirring constantly, until thickened. Garnish with chopped parsley. Serves 6 to 8.

PEARS WITH GRENADINE

8 to 16 canned pear halves, or
4 to 8 fresh pears, pared, cored, and halved
½ cup sugar
2 cups water
¼ cup Grenadine syrup
   Juice of 1 lemon

Combine all ingredients except pears in a saucepan. Heat until sugar is dissolved. Add the pears and poach over medium heat about 8 minutes, turning gently while cooking. Remove pears to serving dish. Cook the sauce vigorously until it has reduced almost to a jelly, about 30 minutes. Pour over the pears and serve either warm or chilled. Serves 8.

BAGUETTES FLAMAND

½ cup butter
¼ cup sugar
   Yolks of 2 hard-cooked eggs
¼ teaspoon almond extract
1 cup flour, sifted
   Grated almonds
2 1-ounce squares semisweet chocolate, melted

Preheat oven to 350°. Cream the butter and sugar. Add the yolks and mix thoroughly. Add the almond extract and flour. Spoon the dough into a pastry bag and press out into baton shapes onto a greased, floured cookie sheet. Sprinkle with grated almonds and bake 8 to 10 minutes. When cool, dip one end of each baton into the melted sweet chocolate and then into some more grated almonds. If desired, chopped pistachio nuts may be substituted for the grated almonds.
Makes 24 to 30.

Dinner for VIPs

CONSOMMÉ DOUBLE   PARMESAN CHIPS

BEEF FILET   POTATOES FLAMAND

INDIVIDUAL SPINACH SOUFFLÉS

CHEESECAKE

PINOT NOIR (CALIFORNIA) OR POMMARD (FRENCH)

Any VIP would be honored by this superb dinner. Combining beef and chicken consommés brings a new taste sensation to your dining. The crusty Parmesan chips are a just right accompaniment. Your beef filet will emerge triumphant with its Madeira sauce flavored with the unusual green peppercorns. Brown, crisp potatoes Flamand and classy spinach soufflés round out a beautiful dinner plate. Close the evening with the creamiest cheesecake you've ever had melt in your mouth and your guests will vote you the VIP!

CONSOMMÉ DOUBLE

3 cups Chicken-flavored Consommé
   (see Basics, page 168)
3 cups Beef-flavored Consommé
   (see Basics, page 168)
1 tablespoon dry sherry
1 tablespoon chopped fresh parsley

Combine the chicken and beef consommés and simmer for 10 minutes to blend the flavors. Just before serving, remove from the heat and add the sherry. Ladle into cups to be served in the living room. Drop a few parsley flakes into each cup. Pass Parmesan chips. Serves 6 to 8.

PARMESAN CHIPS

1 loaf snack rye bread, thinly sliced
½ cup Parmesan cheese, grated
½ cup butter, melted

Place the rye bread slices in a single layer on a cookie sheet and leave out overnight to dry. They will curl up as they dry. Paint both sides with the melted butter and dip in the grated cheese. Spread on a cookie sheet and bake in a preheated 350° oven for 10 minutes. These will keep well in a tightly covered container.

BEEF FILET

2 to 2¾ pounds beef tenderloin
1 cup Beef Stock (see Basics, page 168)
½ cup dry Madeira
2 tablespoons green peppercorns, bottled
   in water, drained
1 tablespoon butter

Allow about ⅓ pound beef tenderloin for each serving. Have your butcher cut the tenderloin into individual filets or do it yourself. If the tenderloin is not large in diameter, you may want to cut the filets a little thicker and pound

them lightly between 2 sheets of waxed paper for a wider looking filet.

Just before you are ready to serve, heat 1 or 2 skillets over fairly high heat. When a drop of water will sizzle in the pans, swirl 1 tablespoon butter quickly around each one, add the filets, and sauté quickly, about 2 or 3 minutes on each side. Do not overcook since they should be served fairly rare. Remove to a heated platter while you prepare the sauce.

Deglaze the skillets with the beef stock, cooking and stirring to scrape up all the tiny beef bits in the pans. Combine into 1 of the pans. Add the Madeira and cook rapidly over high heat, stirring frequently, until the sauce becomes thick and syrupy. Stir in peppercorns. Remove from heat. Whisk in the butter, bit by bit. Pour about 1 tablespoon of the sauce over each filet and serve. Serves 6 to 8.

POTATOES FLAMAND

3 or 4 Idaho potatoes
   Salt
¼ cup butter

Peel the potatoes and slice lengthwise into ¾-inch slices. With a sharp knife, score a diamond pattern on 1 side of each slice. Heat a jelly roll pan and melt the butter in it. Preheat the oven to 350°. Dredge the scored side of the potatoes in the butter, turn and lay unscored side down in the pan. Salt lightly. Bake 45 minutes, turning occasionally, until golden. Serves 6 to 8.

INDIVIDUAL SPINACH SOUFFLÉS

1 10-ounce package frozen
  chopped spinach
1 tablespoon butter
1 tablespoon flour
  Dash ground red pepper (cayenne)
  Dash nutmeg
  Salt
3 tablespoons butter
3 tablespoons flour
1¼ cups milk
4 eggs, separated
  Parmesan cheese, grated

Cook the spinach according to package directions. Drain and squeeze out as much water as possible. Melt 1 tablespoon butter in a skillet and sauté the spinach until it is quite dry. Sprinkle with 1 tablespoon flour and toss to mix thoroughly. Season well with the red pepper, nutmeg, and salt.

Preheat the oven to 350°. Melt 3 tablespoons butter in a saucepan and add the 3 tablespoons flour, stirring briskly to make a smooth roux. Add the milk and cook, stirring, until quite thick. Beat the egg yolks and add a small amount of the white sauce to the eggs; then add this mixture to the white sauce. Fold in the spinach.

Beat the egg whites until stiff but not dry. Stir a small amount of the whites into the spinach mixture to lighten it, and then gently fold in the remaining egg whites, being careful not to overwork them and break them down.

Butter 8 individual soufflé dishes or tin molds and sprinkle with a little grated Parmesan cheese. Fill ⅔ full with the soufflé, place in a pan of hot water, and bake, uncovered, about 15 to 20 minutes. Unmold onto the individual plates with the filet. Serves 8.

CHEESECAKE

16 zwieback crackers
½ cup butter, melted
8 ounces cream cheese
⅔ cup sugar
2 eggs
  Dash salt
2 teaspoons vanilla
1 tablespoon rum
1 cup sour cream
½ cup sugar
1 teaspoon vanilla

Preheat oven to 300°. Using a blender or food processor, reduce the zwieback crackers to fairly fine crumbs. Combine the crumbs with the melted butter. Press this mixture into 2 9-inch pie tins. (Be sure to use pie tins rather than springform pans for this cheesecake.) Bake 5 minutes. Cool.

Cream the cream cheese with ⅔ cup sugar. Add the eggs and salt and beat until smooth. Add 2 teaspoons vanilla and the rum. Pour into the cooled crusts and bake 15 minutes at 300°. Cool on racks for about 20 minutes.

Blend the sour cream with ½ cup sugar and 1 teaspoon vanilla. Spread on the cheesecakes and bake another 5 minutes at 300°. Cool before serving. Serves 12.

An Elegant Dinner

ASPARAGUS HOLLANDAISE

LAMP CHOPS PAPILLOTE   RICE À LA GRECQUE

GRAPES WITH SOUR CREAM

PETIT GAMAY (CALIFORNIA)

OR CÔTE DU RHONE (FRENCH)

The flavor, scent, and look of spring greet you here. Asparagus, peeled, is dressed with hollandaise. Lamb chops are baked in parchment with savory ham and mushrooms. Slit the packages open just before bringing to the table, and they emerge, sauce on top. Rice à la Grecque is brightened with young green peas, fresh mushrooms, crunchy walnuts, and pimiento; add some shredded lettuce just before serving. Green grapes, marinated in Cointreau and topped with sour cream and brown sugar, make one of the most delectable fruit desserts I know.

ASPARAGUS HOLLANDAISE

3 **pounds asparagus**
   Salt
   **Hollandaise Sauce (see Basics,
   page 172)**

Wash the asparagus under running water, snapping off lower ends and making sure there is no sand trapped in the tips. With a vegetable peeler, remove the outer peel below the tips. This is most easily accomplished by laying the spear flat on a board and running the peeler down the length of it; rotate it a little and repeat. Place the spears in a large skillet with the tips pointing outward and the bases toward the center so that they receive the most intense heat. (This way the tips and the less tender bases will cook in the same length of time.) Add salted water to nearly cover and bring to a boil quickly. Simmer just until tender when pierced with a sharp knife or cake tester. Drain and divide equally among the serving plates. Spoon a wide ribbon of hollandaise sauce over the center of each sheaf and serve quickly. Pass remaining sauce. Serves 6 to 8.

LAMB CHOPS PAPILLOTE

½ **pound fresh mushrooms**
2 **tablespoons butter**
½ **cup onion, chopped**
2 **shallots, chopped**
   Salt
   Pepper
1 **tablespoon cognac or brandy**
8 **lamb rib chops 1¼ to 1½ inch thick**
1 **tablespoon olive oil**
8 **thin slices ham**
8 **pieces parchment paper**
   Parsley, chopped

Thoroughly clean and trim the mushrooms and chop finely. Put them in a cloth and twist tightly to extract as much liquid as possible. Sauté the onion and shallots in the butter. When very lightly browned, add the mushrooms, salt, and pepper. Cook, stirring constantly, over medium heat until all moisture is exhausted. Add the cognac or brandy and continue cooking until the moisture has again evaporated. This "mushroom hash" is called *duxelles*. It may be made hours or even days ahead.

Brown chops in the olive oil in a heavy skillet, about 2 minutes on each side. Transfer to dish to cool. Cut heart shapes, about 10x13 inches, from the pieces of parchment paper. Butter the top side of the heart. Fold to mark the center and then lay flat. Along the fold on one half of the heart, lay a slice of ham. Top with a spoonful of duxelles and then a lamb chop. Add another spoonful of duxelles. Fold the other half of the heart over the chop and seal the edge by folding double and crimping, securing with paper clips if necessary. Twist the bottom tip. Repeat with the remaining chops. (They may be prepared ahead to this point and baked just before serving.)

Preheat oven to 450°. Oil a baking sheet lightly and place the envelopes on it. Brush the tops of the paper with oil and bake for 15 minutes, until the envelopes are puffed and brown. Place on heated plates and slit just before bringing to the table. Sprinkle a little freshly chopped parsley in the opening. Serves 8.

RICE À LA GRECQUE

    1 small onion, diced
    2 tablespoons oil
 1½ cups long grain rice, uncooked
    3 cups Chicken Stock (see Basics,
        page 168)
    1 teaspoon salt
    1 10-ounce package frozen peas, thawed
    1 tablespoon chopped pimiento
 ¼ cup chopped walnuts
 ½ cup sliced mushrooms, sautéed in butter
    1 cup shredded lettuce

In a flameproof baking dish, sauté the onion in the oil until soft and transparent but not brown. Add the rice and toss to coat with the oil. Add the chicken stock and salt and bring to a boil. Then either turn heat to low, cover, and cook for 20 minutes, or bake at 350° for 20 minutes. Add the peas, pimiento, walnuts, and mushrooms, and cook for another 5 minutes. Just before serving, add the shredded lettuce and toss lightly with 2 forks. Serves 6 to 8.

GRAPES WITH SOUR CREAM

    2 pounds green seedless grapes
 ½ cup Cointreau
    2 cups sour cream
    1 cup brown sugar

Wash the grapes carefully and remove the stems. Place in individual glass serving dishes and pour the Cointreau over them. Cover with sour cream and sprinkle evenly with brown sugar. Pat down lightly. Refrigerate at least 3 hours. Serves 6 to 8.

First Catch a Duck

BROCCOLI VINAIGRETTE DELUXE

DUCK WITH ORANGE SAUCE   WILD RICE PILAF

PINEAPPLE PARFAIT   PALETS DE DAMES

ZINFANDEL (CALIFORNIA)

OR CHÂTEAUNEUF-DU-PAPE (FRENCH)

You'll catch a lot of compliments, too, with this meal. Begin with broccoli with hot vinaigrette sauce deluxe, featuring pimiento, raw carrots, chopped scallions, and sweet pickle relish. The very special duck with orange sauce is set off perfectly by wild rice pilaf. Conclude the meal in a fitting manner with pineapple parfait and unusual small French cakes, palets de dames.

BROCCOLI VINAIGRETTE DELUXE

4   pounds fresh broccoli
1   cup Vinaigrette Deluxe
      (see Basics, page 173)

Make vinaigrette deluxe according to the directions in Basics. Cover the broccoli with cold water and soak for 10 minutes. Drain well. Remove the large leaves and peel the stalk with a vegetable peeler. Cut the stalks into serving-sized pieces, cutting deep gashes in the lower part of the stalks so that they will cook in the same length of time as the more tender tops. Lay the stalks flat in a large skillet and barely cover with unsalted water. Bring quickly to the boil and simmer, uncovered, until just tender, about 12 minutes. While broccoli is cooking, heat the vinaigrette in a small saucepan. Drain broccoli and immediately pour the hot sauce over. Serves 6 to 8.

DUCK WITH ORANGE SAUCE

2   5- to 6-pound ducklings
2   small onions
2   small ribs celery
2   orange quarters
     Salt
     Pepper
1   cup dry white wine
6   oranges
3   tablespoons sugar
2   tablespoons vinegar
4   prunes
2   tablespoons orange marmalade
1   cup Chicken Stock (see Basics,
      page 168)

Preheat oven to 500°. Wipe the ducks with a damp cloth. Season the cavities with salt and pepper and place an onion, celery rib, and orange quarter inside each. Truss the ducks and rub the outsides with salt and pepper.

Roast for 15 minutes; then reduce heat to 350° and roast about 1 hour, basting frequently with the wine.

Either while the duck is roasting, or early in the day, use a zester or vegetable peeler to remove the zest, or peel, from 3 of the oranges. Cut the zest into fine julienne strips. Squeeze these oranges, reserving the juice. Place the zest in a small pan, cover with drain, cover with fresh water, and boil again for 5 minutes. Repeat this process one more time; drain and reserve.

Melt the sugar over medium high heat in a small, heavy pan until it turns golden brown. Watch carefully to prevent burning. Remove from the heat and carefully add the vinegar, stirring. Set aside.

Peel the remaining 3 oranges, slice, and remove any seeds. Soak the prunes in hot water to soften and plump them. Drain them and stuff with the orange marmalade. Using attelets if you have them, or bamboo skewers, thread an orange slice, a prune, and another orange slice on each of four skewers. Reserve these for later use as garnish.

When the ducks are done, remove them from the pan and keep warm while making the orange sauce. Degrease the pan and add the chicken stock and the juice from the zested oranges. Now add the caramel and orange zest and cook slowly over medium to low heat for 15 minutes. While the sauce is cooking, place the garnish skewers under the broiler and broil until hot and bubbly. Pour the sauce into a gravy boat and pass the sauce at the table with the duck.

Arrange some of the remaining orange slices around the ducks on the platter and thrust the skewers at angles into the ducks for a dramatic presentation. Serves 6 to 8.

WILD RICE PILAF

1 cup long grain rice, uncooked
1 cup wild rice
3 tablespoons oil
1 small onion, minced
4 cups Chicken Stock (see Basics, page 168)
1 clove garlic, peeled
1 stick cinnamon
8 whole cloves
1 blade star anise, optional
½ cup filberts, toasted, skinned, and chopped
2 tablespoons butter

Cover the wild rice with boiling water and soak at least 2 hours. Prepare filberts by toasting in a 375° oven for 8 to 10 minutes. Rub briskly in a rough cloth to remove the dry skins and chop coarsely.

Preheat oven to 350°. Heat the oil in a flameproof casserole and sauté the onion until soft and transparent but not brown. Add the white rice and toss until the rice is well coated with oil. Pour on the chicken stock. Drain the wild rice and add to the casserole, along with the garlic (stuck on a toothpick), cinnamon, cloves, and star anise, if desired. Cover and either bake or cook on top of the stove over low heat for 25 minutes. All liquid should be absorbed.

Remove the spices and garlic. Toss gently with 2 forks to expel the steam. Just before serving, stir in the filberts and butter. Serves 6 to 8.

PINEAPPLE PARFAIT

1 quart lemon sherbet
1 12-ounce jar pineapple ice-cream topping
2 tablespoons orange liqueur
8 whipped cream rosettes

To make the rosettes, force sweetened whipped cream through a pastry tube, fitted with the star tip, onto a cookie sheet. Freeze.

Make small balls of sherbet. Mix the topping with the liqueur. Fill parfait glasses, alternating balls of sherbet with spoonfuls of topping. Top with a rosette. Serves 8.

PALETS DE DAMES

2 tablespoons currants
1 tablespoon rum
¼ cup butter
¼ cup superfine sugar
1 egg
½ cup flour
Dash salt

Soak the currants in the rum for at least 1 hour. Preheat the oven to 350°. Butter and flour a cookie sheet.

Cream the butter and sugar. Add the egg; then the flour and salt. Carefully stir in the currants. Form small round cookies by dropping dough from a teaspoon onto prepared sheets. Bake about 8 minutes, watching carefully. Do not overbake. Makes 24.

Dinner at Eight (A Sit-Down Buffet)

MOSELLE   SALTED HOT PECANS

**PORK CHOPS EN BROCHETTE
WITH BREAD STUFFING**

CURRIED PINEAPPLE

BRUSSELS SPROUTS WITH CELERY SAUCE

BABAS AU RHUM FLAMBÉS

Here's a dinner that is hearty and different. You'll remember this unusual combination. Celery sauce sets off the Brussels sprouts, and the pork chops, lined up on the skewer and garnished with pineapple, orange slices, and watermelon pickles make a dramatic buffet presentation. Babas au rhum, served flambé or not, will give a memorable climax. Furthermore, they are just as good made the day before, maybe even better.

MOSELLE

Have your wine expert select a good German Moselle and serve it chilled as an apéritif. Pass salted hot pecans. Also serve Moselle with the entrée.

PORK CHOPS EN BROCHETTE
WITH BREAD STUFFING

8   to 16 pork rib chops, depending on size
1   small onion, chopped
1   rib celery, chopped
1   tablespoon butter
1   8-ounce package seasoned
    bread stuffing
1¼ cups Chicken Stock (see Basics,
    page 168)
    Salt
    Pepper
    Herbes de Provence (see Basics,
    page 177)
2   oranges, sliced
1   bunch parsley
    Curried Pineapple (recipe follows)
    Watermelon pickles

Preheat oven to 375°. Sauté onion and celery in butter until tender. Combine with bread stuffing and stock. Season to taste with salt, pepper, and herbes de Provence. Shape into balls approximately 2 inches in diameter.

Leave the fat on the chops to baste the rack as it bakes. On long skewers, alternate pork chops, fat side up, in the manner of a standing rack of pork, with balls of stuffing. Season generously with salt, pepper, and herbes de Provence. Place on a rack over a pan of hot water. Shape leftover stuffing into balls and bake on a greased cookie sheet along with the meat. Bake until the internal temperature of the pork registers 185° on a meat thermometer, about 1 hour.

Place the skewers on a heated platter and surround with additional balls of stuffing. Arrange 2 or 3 balls of extra stuffing on each of 2 or more skewers, alternating with orange slices and sprigs of parsley. Stab skewers diagonally into pork racks. Arrange the remaining orange slices, curried pineapple slices, watermelon pickles, and sprigs of parsley in a decorative manner around the pork. Guests may then help themselves to 1 or 2 pork chops and some stuffing balls, pulling them off the skewers. Serves 8.

CURRIED PINEAPPLE

1   16-ounce can sliced pineapple
½   cup dry white wine
¼   cup sugar
2   teaspoons curry powder

Drain the pineapple. Pour the juice into a skillet and add the wine, sugar, and curry powder. Bring to a boil, add pineapple slices, and simmer 8 minutes. Refrigerate overnight to blend flavors. Serves 8.

BRUSSELS SPROUTS WITH CELERY SAUCE

2   pounds Brussels sprouts
1   cup Chicken Stock (see Basics,
    page 168)
1   rib celery, chopped fine
½   cup Chicken Stock
1   cup Béchamel Sauce (see Basics,
    page 170)
1   tablespoon parsley, chopped

Wash Brussels sprouts carefully, removing discolored outer leaves. Make a small *X* in the stem end of each sprout with a sharp knife tip so that the dense base will cook as quickly as the tender outer part. Place in a saucepan with the 1 cup chicken stock and bring to a boil. Cook, covered, about 15 minutes or until just tender. Meanwhile, cook the chopped celery in the remaining ½ cup stock, uncovered, about 5 minutes, or until tender crisp. Drain, reserving cooking liquid. Make béchamel sauce and thin with some of the stock used for cooking the celery. Add the celery to the sauce. Drain the Brussels sprouts and place in serving dish. Top with the celery sauce and sprinkle with the chopped parsley. Serves 6 to 8.

BABAS AU RHUM FLAMBÉS

    1 package dry yeast
    ¼ cup warm water (105°-115°)
       Pinch sugar
    2 eggs
    1½ cups flour
    ¼ cup warm milk
    ¼ pound butter, softened
    1 teaspoon salt
    2 tablespoons sugar
    1 cup Simple Syrup (see Basics, page 188)
    2 tablespoons rum
    ¼ cup rum

Dissolve the yeast in the warm water, adding the pinch of sugar. Beat the eggs and add the flour and warm milk. Stir in the yeast mixture. Work with a wooden spoon until the dough becomes elastic. Cover and let rise in a warm place until double, about 1½ hours.

Cut the butter into 8 to 10 small pieces and add one at a time to the dough, working it in a slapping motion with a rubber scraper. Be sure that all the butter is incorporated into the dough. Add the salt and sugar and mix well.

Preheat oven to 425°. Thoroughly grease 12 baba or ⅓- to ½-cup tin molds. Fill each of the molds half full of dough. Set in a warm place and let rise until double. Bake about 12 minutes. Remove the babas from the molds.

While the babas are baking, make the simple syrup according to the directions in Basics. Remove from heat and stir in the 2 tablespoons rum. Divide the syrup among the molds and return the warm babas to the molds to soak up the syrup. To serve, turn out all the babas onto a serving platter. Warm ¼ cup rum in a small pan, light with a match, and pour the flaming rum over the babas. Serve immediately.

A Dinner to Please the Menfolks

CONSOMMÉ WITH AVOCADO

BEEF RIB ROAST   SWISS CHEESE POTATOES

GREEN SALAD

CHOCOLATE MOUSSE À LA VERNA

PINOT NOIR (CALIFORNIA)

OR POMMARD (FRENCH)

After more than forty years teaching experience, I have found that there are certain foods that never fail to win men's hearts—and stomachs. Here they make up the entire menu. Clear consommé, sherry and avocado added, begins this evocative dinner. The rib roast needs nothing except roasting to medium rare. The very special potatoes are unmolded and served masked in sour cream with driblets of melting Swiss cheese cascading down the sides. My extraordinary chocolate mousse may just possibly be the smoothest and creamiest you have ever tasted.

CONSOMMÉ WITH AVOCADO

1 avocado, not too ripe
Ascorbic acid solution (2 cups water and
1 ascorbic acid tablet) or 2 tablespoons
lemon juice
4 to 6 cups Consommé (see Basics,
page 168)
2 to 3 tablespoons dry sherry, if desired

Peel and pit avocado. Cut into cubes or shape into balls. Place pieces in a bowl and immerse in ascorbic acid solution or sprinkle with lemon juice to prevent darkening. Cover tightly and refrigerate. Heat consommé. Just before serving, remove from heat and add the sherry, if desired. Pour into cups and add a few pieces of avocado to each serving. Serves 6 to 8.

BEEF RIB ROAST

1 standing rib roast of quality beef
(3 to 4 pounds)
Salt
Pepper

Bring beef to room temperature. Sprinkle with salt and pepper. Place fat side up on rack of shallow roaster. Preheat oven to 375°. Place the roast in the oven and roast 1 hour. Turn off the heat but *do not open the oven door.* There must be an interval of at least 2 hours before the heat is turned on again. Now turn on the oven to 375° again and cook the roast 35 minutes for rare, 45 minutes for medium, and 50 minutes for well done. Serves 6 to 8.

SWISS CHEESE POTATOES

8 medium potatoes, peeled
4 tablespoons butter
1 teaspoon salt
¼ teaspoon white pepper
2 cups grated Swiss cheese
¾ cup sour cream

Cube the potatoes and cook in boiling salted water until tender, about 15 minutes. Drain and mash. Add the butter, salt, and pepper and stir into a firm mixture. Generously butter a 1½-quart Charlotte mold or 2-pound coffee can. Line bottom with a layer of potatoes and dot with additional butter and some of the grated cheese. Continue alternating potatoes with butter and cheese, using 1½ cups of the cheese, until mold is filled. This can be done early in the day.

Preheat oven to 350°. Bake the potatoes until they are heated and the cheese melts, about 30 minutes. Invert the mold onto an ovenproof serving plate. Spread the sour cream on the top, allowing some to drip down the sides. Sprinkle with remaining ½ cup of cheese on the top. Place under the broiler very briefly to melt the cheese. Serve immediately. Serves 6 to 8.

GREEN SALAD

See "A Dinner for Good Friends," page 127.

CHOCOLATE MOUSSE À LA VERNA

½ pound semisweet chocolate
½ cup sugar
¼ cup water
5 eggs, separated
1 teaspoon vanilla
3 tablespoons Crème de Menthe, if desired
Crème Chantilly (see Basics, page 187)

Melt the chocolate with the sugar and water in the top of a double boiler over simmering water. Stir until smooth, remove from heat, and cool to room temperature. Quickly whisk in the yolks and then the vanilla. Beat the whites to soft peaks and fold gently into the chocolate mixture. Pour into a serving dish or individual pots de crème and chill overnight. If desired, place a few drops of Crème de Menthe on the top of each serving and allow to seep down into the mousse to flavor it. If using the individual pots, top each serving with a small amount of crème Chantilly before serving. Otherwise, pass the crème Chantilly. Serves 6 to 8.

Suppers and Informal Entertaining

Truly French

BOURRIDE FRENCH BREAD

GREEN SALAD

PEACHES WITH RASPBERRY SAUCE

French, and intended for the hardy diner who appreciates garlic, is this bourride, a fish concoction fragrant with herbs and the most unforgettable of sauces, aïoli. Yes, you really *do* use five cloves of garlic! The bourride is served with crusty French bread and followed by a refreshing green salad. For dessert, what could be better than gently poached peaches bathed in a ruby red raspberry sauce?

BOURRIDE

2 pounds white fish (cod, haddock,
    bass, or flounder)
    Salt
    Pepper
1 onion, minced
    Bouquet Garni (see Basics, page 177)
    Pinch thyme
    Pinch fennel seeds
1 cup clam juice
3 cups water
12 slices firm white bread, crusts removed
1 clove garlic, halved
2 cups Aïoli Sauce (see Basics, page 175)

Cut the fish into serving pieces and season
with salt and pepper. Place in a Dutch oven
or soup pot. Cover with minced onion and
add the bouquet garni, thyme, and fennel.
Add the clam juice and water. Cover, bring to
a quick boil, reduce heat, and simmer for 10
minutes.

Toast the bread and rub each slice with the
cut end of garlic. Prepare the aïoli sauce.
Remove fish from broth and keep warm in the
oven. Strain the broth. Little by little,
combine 3 cups of the broth with 1 cup aïoli
sauce. Mix carefully and heat in the top of a
double boiler until it coats the spoon. *Do not
boil*.

Put toast in a soup tureen and pour the
sauce over it. Serve the fish on the side. Pass
extra aïoli sauce. Serves 6 to 8.

FRENCH BREAD

See Basics, page 180.

GREEN SALAD

See "A Dinner for Good Friends," page 127.

PEACHES WITH RASPBERRY SAUCE

2 15-ounce cans white peaches
    (regular peaches may be substituted)
¼ cup sugar
    Vanilla bean
2 cups Raspberry Sauce (see Basics,
    page 189)

Drain peaches, reserving syrup. Combine the
syrup and sugar, and add the vanilla bean.
Heat in a skillet until sugar is dissolved. Drop
in peaches and poach gently for 8 minutes.
Remove peaches to serving dishes. Combine
remaining syrup with the raspberry sauce.
Pour over peaches. Chill well. Serves 6 to 8.

A Salad Buffet

RAPHAEL   DRY ROASTED PEANUTS

SALAD BUFFET

SPICE CAKE WITH LEMON FROSTING

SEMILLON

This salad buffet is guest's choice—you fix the fixings and guests design their own salad. Give them plenty of fresh vegetables to choose from and add the marinated garbanzo beans for a change of texture. Julienne strips of salami or ham and white meat of chicken or turkey make a hearty main course salad.

This menu also solves a dilemma—since wine does not go well with vinegar and is never served with salad, and you still like wine, what do you do? Serve Raphael, a French apéritif, with dry roasted peanuts as an appetizer, and Semillon, a semisweet wine, with your dessert, which is a delicate spice cake with lemon frosting.

SALAD BUFFET

- 3 assorted lettuces
- 1 15-ounce can garbanzo beans
- ½ pound hard salami or ham, cut julienne
- ½ pound cooked white meat of chicken or turkey, cut julienne
- 1 green pepper, cut in ½-inch squares
- 1 bunch radishes, sliced
- 1 pint cherry tomatoes, halved
- ½ cup green onions, thinly sliced
- ½ cup parsley, chopped
  Vinaigrette Sauce (see Basics, page 173)
  Mayonnaise Verte (see Basics, page 175)
  Russian Dressing (see Basics, page 175)

Wash and dry the lettuce and tear into a large salad bowl. Drain and rinse the garbanzo beans. Place in a saucepan and cover with water. Bring quickly to a boil. Drain again and marinate in a small amount of vinaigrette sauce.

Place each ingredient except the lettuces and vinaigrette sauce in small bowls. Just before serving, toss the lettuce with a small amount of vinaigrette sauce and set the salad bowl in the center of the buffet. Surround with the small bowls of garnishes and mayonnaise verte and Russian dressing. Serves 6 to 8.

SPICE CAKE

- ½ cup butter
- 1 cup brown sugar
- 2 eggs
- 1½ cups cake flour
- ½ teaspoon baking soda
- ½ teaspoon baking powder
- ½ teaspoon cloves
- ½ teaspoon cinnamon
- ¼ teaspoon salt
- ½ cup buttermilk

Preheat oven to 325°. Grease and flour a 7x10-inch cake pan or a pan of equivalent size.

Cream the butter with the brown sugar and add the eggs. Beat well. Sift the dry ingredients together and add to the creamed mixture alternately with the buttermilk. Pour into the prepared pan and bake 35 minutes or until it tests done with a cake tester inserted in the center. Cool and spread with Lemon Frosting. Cut in diamond shapes to serve. Serves 8 to 10.

LEMON FROSTING

- ¼ cup butter, melted
- 2 tablespoons lemon juice
  Grated rind of 1 lemon
- 1 tablespoon cream
- 2 cups powdered sugar, sifted

Combine all ingredients to make a smooth spread. Add more powdered sugar if desired to make a thicker frosting.

A Simple Elegance

SOAVE (ITALIAN)

ONION SANDWICHES   CUCUMBER ROUNDS

STEAK DIANE   BROCCOLI AND CAULIFLOWER

PEARS WITH MERINGUE AND CHOCOLATE SAUCE

CABERNET SAUVIGNON (CALIFORNIA) OR

VALPOLICELLA (ITALIAN)

Polish your chafing dish for a dramatic flambé—steak Diane, prepared at the table. Filet is cut thin, sautèed in butter and oil, flavored with shallots and a little Dijon mustard and Worcestershire sauce, and simmered in red wine and beef stock. Drench it with warmed brandy and light for a shimmering flame. Broccoli and cauliflower team up to make a nice color combination. Pears, poached, tinted with apricot, and topped with meringue and chocolate sauce, make a lovely finale to an elegant meal.

ONION SANDWICHES

Thin-sliced firm white bread
Butter
Small sweet onions, about 1 inch
in diameter
Salt
Pepper
Mayonnaise (see Basics, page 174)
Parsley, chopped
Paprika

Cut thin-sliced bread into 1½-inch rounds. Spread with butter. Cut the onions into very thin slices and place on half the bread rounds, 1 slice per round. Sprinkle with salt and pepper. Top with the remaining rounds. Roll the edges of the sandwiches first in mayonnaise and then in either chopped parsley or paprika. Chill for several hours before serving.

CUCUMBER ROUNDS

1   **seedless European cucumber**
     Vinaigrette Sauce (see Basics, page 173)
     Thin-sliced firm white bread
     Herb Butter (see Basics, page 177)

Score the cucumber lengthwise with the tines of a fork to give a scalloped edge. Slice thinly and marinate at least 30 minutes in some vinaigrette sauce. Just before serving, cut 1½-inch rounds from the bread and spread with herb butter. Top each bread round with a drained cucumber slice.

STEAK DIANE

8   **slices firm white bread or French bread**
     Butter
¼   **cup oil**
8   **tenderloin steaks, ½ inch thick**
¼   **cup butter**
¼   **cup chopped shallots or scallions**
     Salt
     Pepper
1   **cup dry red wine**
1   **cup Beef Stock (see Basics, page 168)**
½   **tablespoon or more Dijon mustard**
½   **tablespoon or more Worcestershire sauce**
¼   **cup Cognac**
1   **tablespoon cornstarch mixed with**
1   **tablespoon water**
¼   **cup parsley, chopped**

Note: Although this dish is really not complicated, timing is important. A practice session for the family might be a wise idea before you try preparing it in front of your guests.

Cut the bread in 3-inch rounds and butter both sides. Sauté until golden brown. These croutons can be prepared early in the day and reheated in a 350° oven for about 5 minutes.

Pound the steaks gently between 2 sheets of waxed paper to about half their original thickness. Have all the remaining ingredients ready on a tray to have handy at the table. Use an electric skillet or chafing dish.

Heat the oil and sauté the steaks lightly on both sides. Roll to keep warm and remove to a separate dish. Add the butter to the pan and sauté the chopped shallots. Add salt, pepper, the wine, and the stock. Stir in the mustard and Worcestershire sauce and simmer 2 or 3 minutes. Return the steaks to the pan and heat them, turning once. Warm the Cognac in a separate pan, light it, and pour it, flaming, over the steaks. Stir in the cornstarch mixture and cook, stirring until the sauce thickens.

Place the steaks on the croutons, top with sauce, and sprinkle with chopped parsley. Pass remaining sauce. Serves 8.

BROCCOLI AND CAULIFLOWER

1 **large bunch broccoli**
1 **large head cauliflower**
   Salt
   Pepper
¼ **cup butter, melted**

Trim the broccoli, peeling the lower stems with a vegetable peeler. Separate into slender stalks of even size. Place in 1 layer in a large skillet with the flowerettes pointing out so that they receive less heat and cook more slowly than the stems. Add about ½-inch water and sprinkle with salt. Cook until just tender crisp. Remove from pan with kitchen tongs to paper toweling to drain.

Wash the cauliflower and separate into small flowerettes. Bring about 1 cup salted water to boil in a saucepan large enough to hold the cauliflower and drop in the flowerettes. Cook just until tender crisp. Drain on paper toweling.

Arrange the 2 vegetables on a serving platter, either combined or separated and drizzle with the melted butter. Sprinkle with salt and pepper. If done ahead of time, cover with a piece of buttered waxed paper and reheat in a 350° oven for 8 to 10 minutes. Serves 6 to 8.

PEARS WITH MERINGUE AND CHOCOLATE SAUCE

8 **pear halves**
3 **tablespoons apricot jam**
¼ **cup sugar**
   Juice and grated rind of 1 lemon
¼ **cup pear juice**
1 **recipe Meringue (see Basics, page 187)**
2 **ounces semisweet chocolate**

Combine the apricot jam, sugar, lemon juice and rind, and pear juice to make a syrup. Bring to a boil, carefully drop in the pear halves, and simmer about 8 minutes. Cool in the syrup. Working carefully to avoid breaking the pears, remove them from the syrup, and place them round side up, in a baking pan. Reserve syrup.

Preheat oven to 425°. Prepare meringue according to the directions in Basics and blanket each pear half with it. Bake the pears for about 5 minutes, until the meringue is browned. Remove to individual dishes. Melt the chocolate in the reserved syrup. Pour around the meringue pears just before serving. Serves 8.

In the Meyer Manner

SHRIMP OR SNAILS IN GARLIC BUTTER

FRENCH BREAD   SALAD EMELINE

LEMON CREAM CHEESECAKE

WHITE OR RED BURGUNDY (CALIFORNIA)

If snails are hard to come by, you can use shrimp to begin this dinner. Either is drenched in savory garlic butter and served with plenty of French bread for soaking up the butter. After this, you are ready for salad Emeline, hearty with shreds of cooked ham and chicken, tomato wedges, and its special dressing. Lemon cheesecake in a rich chocolate crust adds a wonderful final touch.

SHRIMP OR SNAILS IN GARLIC BUTTER

48 large shrimp or canned snails
2 cups butter
¼ cup chives, chopped
½ teaspoon salt
½ teaspoon dried tarragon
2 tablespoons shallots, minced
3 cloves garlic, minced
½ cup parsley, minced

Combine the butter with remaining ingredients. Preheat the oven to 400°.

If using shrimp, shell and devein them, and then carefully cut down the back, not quite through. Gently flatten them and place between 2 sheets of waxed paper. Pound lightly with a mallet. Spread them with the butter mixture and close the shrimp. Place one in each depression in individual escargot pans or lay them all in a buttered jelly roll pan. Melt leftover butter mixture and brush on shrimp. Bake 12 minutes or until done.

If using snails, rinse them thoroughly under cold running water and drain. Place a small amount of butter mixture in each escargot shell. Press a snail into each shell, being careful not to wedge it in too tightly. Fill the shell with more garlic butter. Place on the pans, open side up, and bake 12 minutes until hot and bubbly.

Serve with plenty of warm French bread (see Basics, page 180) to dip in the melted escargot butter. Serves 6 to 8.

FRENCH BREAD

See Basics, page 180.

SALAD EMELINE

3 heads assorted lettuce
   Vinaigrette Sauce (see Basics, page 173)
2 tomatoes, peeled and cut in wedges
½ pound cooked white meat of chicken, cut julienne
¼ pound baked ham, cut julienne
1 cucumber, partially peeled and sliced
2 hard-cooked eggs
   Bibb lettuce for garnish
   Emeline Dressing (see Basics, page 174)

Wash and dry lettuce and tear into a large salad bowl. Toss with just enough vinaigrette sauce to moisten each leaf. Line a platter with Bibb lettuce leaves. Pile the lettuce on the platter and garnish lavishly with the tomatoes, chicken, ham, and cucumber. Separate the yolks from the whites of the hard-cooked eggs. Chop the whites finely and force the yolks through a sieve. Sprinkle both the yolks and the whites over the top of the salad. Pass Emeline dressing. Serves 6 to 8.

LEMON CREAM CHEESECAKE

1 8½-ounce package chocolate icebox cookies
¼ cup butter, melted
1 8-ounce package cream cheese, softened
6 tablespoons sugar
1 teaspoon vanilla
   Juice and rind of ½ lemon
2 egg yolks
1 envelope unflavored gelatin
2 tablespoons cold water
3 egg whites
1 cup heavy cream, whipped
1 1-ounce square semisweet chocolate

Process the cookies in a blender or a food processor until they become crumbs. Blend in the melted butter and press into the bottom of a 9-inch springform pan or a loose-bottomed cake pan.

Combine the cream cheese, sugar, vanilla, lemon juice, and grated rind. Beat in the egg yolks. Soak the gelatin in 2 tablespoons cold water to soften and heat gently until dissolved. Add to the cheese mixture. Beat the egg whites until stiff but not dry. Gently fold the whites into the cheese mixture. Fold in the whipped cream. Pile the filling into the crust and chill at least 2 hours. Before serving, grate the semisweet chocolate and sprinkle it around the edge of the cake, reserving a small amount for the center. Serves 8.

To Invite
the Neighbors In

CHICKEN WINGS AND DRUMSTICKS

COLESLAW   COLACHE

WATERMELON

ICE TEA   LEMONADE

This could be a block party or a backyard supper on the patio. It serves as well for large or small groups. Coat chicken wings and drumsticks with tangy mustard and then sour cream, roll in toast crumbs, and bake. These go fast, so you will be well advised to plan on the generous side. Accompany your chicken with a new version of the old favorite, coleslaw. Colache, an herb-flavored combination of zucchini, corn, tomatoes, onions, and green peppers, is perfect for late summer. Top your picnic off with ease and watermelon!

CHICKEN WINGS AND DRUMSTICKS

3 to 5 pounds chicken wings
and drumsticks
¼ cup Dijon mustard
1 cup sour cream
2 cups dry bread crumbs, sifted

The bread crumbs can be easily made in the blender or food processor. The amounts given are approximate and you may need more.

Preheat oven to 350°. Separate the joints of the chicken wings and reserve the tips for stock. Put the mustard, sour cream, and bread crumbs into three separate pie pans. Using your hands, wipe the mustard and then the sour cream on each piece of chicken and then roll it in the crumbs. Place the chicken pieces on lightly oiled cookie sheets or jelly roll pans.

Bake 1 hour in upper level of oven, turning once. These are at their best served at room temperature. Serves 6 to 8.

COLESLAW

1 cup sugar
2 tablespoons water
⅓ cup vinegar
Celery seed, optional
Dash salt
½ medium cabbage, shredded (green or
red cabbage, or half of each)

Place sugar, water, and vinegar in saucepan; heat, stirring, until sugar dissolves. Remove from heat and add celery seed and salt to taste. While still warm, pour dressing over shredded cabbage and let stand about 30 minutes. Chill. Sour cream to taste may be added for a creamy dressing. Serves 6 to 8.

COLACHE

¼ cup oil
1 onion, chopped
1 green pepper, diced
4 zucchini, sliced
3 fresh tomatoes, peeled and chopped
1 teaspoon salt
Pepper
¼ teaspoon basil
Pinch oregano
Pinch chili powder, optional
2 17-ounce cans whole kernel corn, drained

Heat the oil in a large skillet or Dutch oven. Sauté the onion until soft. Add the green pepper and sauté lightly. Now add the zucchini and sauté until soft. Add the tomatoes and seasonings and simmer 20 minutes. Add the corn and heat through. Serves 6 to 8.

From the Five Oaks

SALAD FIVE OAKS

BROCHETTE OF LAMB   CURRY SAUCE

SAFFRON RICE PILAF

COFFEE SOUFFLÉ

PINOT NOIR (CALIFORNIA) OR

BROUILLY BEAUJOLAIS (FRENCH)

One of the most creative menus I have ever found was in a restaurant in Greenwich Village named the Five Oaks after the five magnificent oak trees that stand in the front. This restaurant featured an exceptional mixture of ethnic cuisines, mostly Mediterranean in origin, with unusual flavors that quietly enhance one another. The spicy dressing for the salad is just right for preparing your palate for the ground lamb and curry sauce. The subtle flavoring and brilliant color of the saffron rice pilaf are perfect with these brochettes. And what better way to present coffee than in steaming puffy soufflé?

SALAD FIVE OAKS

1 pound spinach
1 head Romaine lettuce
3 hard-cooked eggs
  Cherry tomato halves
  Vinaigrette Sauce (see Basics, page 173)
  Five Oaks Dressing (recipe follows)

Wash and dry the greens, being careful to remove all stems from the spinach. Tear, do not cut, into bite-sized pieces. Chop the eggs, and in a large bowl, gently toss the eggs and greens with just enough vinaigrette sauce to moisten each leaf. Distribute the salad among individual chilled salad plates and garnish with tomato halves. Top with a dollop of Five Oaks dressing, passing more if desired. Serves 6 to 8.

FIVE OAKS DRESSING

1 cup catsup
¼ cup oil
2 tablespoons wine vinegar (red preferred)
1 teaspoon Worcestershire sauce
2 tablespoons celery, chopped
1 green onion, chopped
2 sprigs parsley, chopped
1 teaspoon sugar
  Dash salt
  Dash pepper
1 teaspoon soy sauce
½ teaspoon dried basil
½ cup shaved ice

Place all ingredients except the ice in a blender or a food processor. Process until well blended. Add the shaved ice to chill quickly, blend briefly, and serve.

BROCHETTE OF LAMB

2 pounds ground lamb
2 slices white bread
¼ cup Beef Stock (see Basics, page 168)
2 eggs, beaten
  Dash salt
  Pepper
½ teaspoon rosemary
2 tablespoons parsley
2 tablespoons onion, grated
½ pound bacon

Preheat oven to 400°. Tear the bread into small pieces and soak in the stock. Combine with remaining ingredients except bacon and form into rather firm balls, making them somewhat oval in shape. Wrap each in half a slice of bacon and secure well with a wooden pick. Thread 2 or 3 on a skewer. Place all the skewers on a rack in a baking pan. If you put a little hot water in the bottom of the pan, it will eliminate the burning of the meat juices, reducing the chance of smoke in the oven. Bake the lamb 30 minutes. Just before serving, brown briefly under the broiler. Serves 6 to 8.

CURRY SAUCE

3 tablespoons butter
1 tablespoon curry powder
2 tablespoons flour
1½ cups Chicken Stock (see Basics, page 168)
  Dash salt

In a heavy saucepan, melt the butter and add the curry powder and flour all at once. Whisk briskly to form a smooth roux. Cook gently over medium heat, whisking constantly. *Do not brown*. Add the chicken stock, stirring constantly, and cook until thickened. Taste for seasoning. Pass with the lamb brochettes.

SAFFRON RICE PILAF

3   tablespoons oil
2   small onions, minced
2   cups long grain rice, uncooked
    Pinch rosemary
4   cups Chicken Stock (see Basics,
    page 168)
1   teaspoon salt
    Pinch saffron
2   tablespoons parsley, chopped
1   green onion, chopped

Preheat oven to 350°. Heat the oil in a skillet and sauté the onion until soft. Add the rice and rosemary and stir gently until all the rice is coated with oil. Transfer the rice to a casserole and add just enough boiling chicken stock to cover the rice to a depth of 1 inch. Add the salt and saffron. Cover and bake about 25 minutes or until all the moisture is absorbed. Toss with 2 forks to expel the steam. Garnish with the parsley and green onion. Serves 6 to 8.

COFFEE SOUFFLÉ

3   tablespoons butter
3   tablespoons flour
½   cup hot milk
½   cup hot strong coffee
4   egg yolks
¼   cup sugar
¼   teaspoon salt
5   egg whites
¼   cup sugar
    Chocolate Sauce (see Basics, page 190)

Note: To make coffee of the strength needed for this recipe, it is suggested that instant coffee be used. There are some mocha-flavored instant coffees on the grocery shelves that are particularly good for this dessert.

Preheat the oven to 375°. Prepare a 1½-quart soufflé dish by buttering the inside and sprinkling it with granulated sugar. Melt the butter in a heavy saucepan and add the flour. Whisking constantly, cook over medium heat to form a smooth roux. Add the milk and coffee and continue cooking and stirring until smooth and thickened. Beat the egg yolks with the first ¼ cup sugar and the salt. Gradually add the milk mixture to the egg yolks and blend thoroughly. Cool a little. Beat the egg whites until stiff but not dry, gradually adding the second ¼ cup sugar. Fold them into the first mixture. Pour into the soufflé dish and bake on the middle shelf of the oven for 35 to 40 minutes. Sprinkle the top with sifted powdered sugar and serve immediately with hot chocolate sauce. Serves 6 to 8.

A Delicatessen Party

SLICED HAM   SAUSAGES   COLD CUTS

BAKED BEANS   POTATO SALAD   COLESLAW

SLICED TOMATOES

VARIETY OF CHEESES   SAUCES FOR MEATS

PICKLES, RELISHES

BREADS   ROLLS

COCONUT CREAM PIE

PECAN PIE   SOUR CREAM PIE

I think one of the best ways to spend New Year's Eve or any other festive occasion is to host a *charcuterie* party. Your party setting should resemble a delicatessen as much as possible. On the tables, place coffee makers and cups, some bottles of beer, and jugs of red and white wines, and wine and beer glasses. Cover your tables with black and white tablecloths and red napkins. Burn some candles in wine bottles; keep kettles of boiling water on the stove for those guests who would like a hot dog or bockwurst. For my own party I borrow a small showcase and place desserts in it.

I suggest your menu include sliced ham and cold cuts, hot dogs, bockwurst (when it's available at Eastertime) or bratwurst, baked beans, potato salad, coleslaw, sliced tomatoes, a variety of cheese, and all kinds of bread and rolls. Don't overlook pickles, pickled beets, catsup, chili sauce, mustards, horseradish, and sliced onions. For dessert, serve cut pieces of homemade pies—pecan, coconut cream, and my sour cream pie.

The recipes for all of these dishes have been included here, but the real beauty of this party is that if time is short, you can buy any or even all of the items on this menu!

BAKED BEANS

    2 pounds dry navy beans
    ¼ pound salt pork
    ¼ cup molasses
    2 tablespoons brown sugar
    1 tablespoon prepared mustard
    1 teaspoon salt
    ½ to 1 cup boiling water
    ½ cup dry sherry

Soak the beans overnight in cold water to cover. Next morning, drain and cover with fresh cold water. Cook at a simmer over medium heat until the skin peels when you blow on a bean held in a spoon, about 30 minutes. Drain and wash with warm water.

Preheat oven to 250°. Put ⅓ of the beans in a large crock and top with some of the salt pork, cut in pieces. Repeat until all the beans are used. Combine the molasses, brown sugar, mustard, and salt and pour over the beans. Cover with boiling water. Cover and bake at least 3 hours. Uncover and taste for salt. Correct seasonings and add the sherry. Bake 1 hour more, uncovered, to brown. Serves 6 to 8.

POTATO SALAD

    3 to 4 pounds red potatoes
       Salt
       Pepper
    2 tablespoons parsley, chopped
    1 bunch green onions, sliced
       Vinaigrette Sauce (see Basics, page 173)
    ¼ cup buttermilk
    1 cup Mayonnaise (see Basics, page 174)
    6 hard-cooked eggs

Drop the potatoes into a pot of boiling, unsalted water. Cook until they test barely done with a cake tester. As each one tests done, remove it from the boiling water and drop into a bowl of ice water to stop the cooking process immediately. The potatoes should remain firm. While the potatoes are still warm, peel and slice them into a bowl. Add salt, pepper, parsley, and green onions. Pour over just enough vinaigrette sauce to moisten and let cool. Whisk the buttermilk into the mayonnaise and gently toss it with the potatoes. Chill well. Just before serving, garnish with sliced hard-cooked eggs. Serves 6 to 8.

COLESLAW

See "To Invite the Neighbors In," page 114.

COCONUT CREAM PIE

    1 baked pie shell (see Basics, page 185)
    1 recipe Pastry Cream (see Basics, page 191)
    1 cup grated fresh coconut or packaged flaked coconut
    1 recipe Meringue (see Basics, page 187)

Bake the pie shell and make the pastry cream according to the directions in Basics, using vanilla for flavoring. Fold in the coconut, reserving about 1 tablespoon for the topping. Preheat oven to 350°.

Make the meringue according to the directions in Basics. Pour the pastry cream into the baked pie shell. Carefully spread the meringue over the filling and sprinkle the top with the reserved coconut. Bake about 15 minutes until golden. Serves 6 to 8.

PECAN PIE

1 unbaked pie shell (see Basics, page 185)
3 eggs
¾ cup sugar
1 cup corn syrup, light or dark
½ teaspoon vanilla
1 cup pecan halves
2 tablespoons butter, melted

Make pastry according to the directions in Basics. Preheat oven to 300°. Beat the eggs until light and add the sugar gradually. Then add the corn syrup and vanilla. Spread the pecan halves over the bottom of the pie crust and cover with the filling. Drizzle with the melted butter. Bake 40 minutes; then raise the oven temperature to 350° and bake another 10 minutes or until the filling is set and a knife or cake tester inserted near the middle comes out clean. Serves 6 to 8.

SOUR CREAM PIE

1 unbaked pie shell (see Basics, page 185)
1 egg
1 cup sugar
1 cup raisins or ⅔ cup chopped pecans
   or walnuts
1 cup sour cream
1 tablespoon vinegar
¼ teaspoon salt
¼ teaspoon cinnamon
¼ teaspoon nutmeg
¼ teaspoon cloves

Preheat oven to 450°. Make pastry according to the directions in Basics. Beat the egg and sugar together until light and the sugar is dissolved. Add remaining ingredients and blend thoroughly. Pour into unbaked pie shell. Bake 45 minutes or until a cake tester inserted in the center comes out clean. Serves 6 to 8.

Not Strictly for Conversation

SHERRY

OLIVES   CURRIED PEANUTS

CHICKEN BONNE FEMME   FRENCH ROLLS

BIBB LETTUCE WITH MUSTARD VINAIGRETTE

APPLES AND PEARS JEANNETTE

CHARDONNAY (CALIFORNIA)

OR GRAVES (FRENCH)

Serve your guests curried peanuts and olives with their sherry, and their conversation will quickly turn to gastronomy. The main course, chicken bonne femme, is fricasseed chicken served with carrots, mushrooms, and tiny peas in a savory sauce. Delicate Bibb lettuce in a dressing subtly flavored with Dijon mustard makes a happy bridge from the chicken to the apples and pears Jeannette. This dessert is so simple to prepare and so delicious that it will quickly become a favorite. It may also be served with whipped cream or ice cream.

CURRIED PEANUTS

2 tablespoons oil
1 8-ounce can cocktail peanuts,
   not dry roasted
2 teaspoons brown sugar
½ teaspoon curry powder, or more

Heat the oil in a heavy skillet. Add the peanuts and brown sugar. Cook over medium heat, shaking pan and keeping peanuts moving with a fork or wooden spoon. Watch carefully to prevent burning. After about 10 minutes, add the curry powder. Stir in carefully. Remove from the heat and drain twice on fresh paper toweling. Break apart. To store, place back in the original can.

CHICKEN BONNE FEMME

2 2½- to 3-pound broiler-fryers, whole
1 tablespoon lemon juice
2 tablespoons butter
2 tablespoons oil
1 carrot, chopped
1 rib celery, chopped
1 onion, chopped
4 sprigs parsley
2 sprigs fresh tarragon or ½ teaspoon dried
½ cup Chicken Stock (see Basics, page 168)
½ cup dry white wine
8 carrots
1 pound fresh mushrooms
1 10-ounce package frozen tiny peas, thawed
   Beurre Manié (see Basics, page 171)
   Parsley, chopped

Preheat the oven to 350°. Rub the chickens with lemon juice. Heat the butter and oil in a heavy, flameproof casserole or cocotte large enough to hold both birds. Sauté them lightly, one at a time, on all sides. Remove from the pan and add the chopped carrot, celery, and onion. Sauté until soft. This mixture of vegetables, which forms a bed for the meat, is called a *mirepoix*. Lay the chickens on the mirepoix and lay the sprigs of parsley and tarragon on the breasts. If using dried tarragon, sprinkle over the breasts. Pour the chicken stock and white wine into the casserole, cover, and bake about 1 hour.

Meanwhile, prepare the vegetables. Peel and slice the carrots. Cook in boiling salted water until *al dente*, about 12 minutes. Clean the mushrooms, flute them if desired, and sauté in butter.

When the chickens are ready, remove to a heated platter and keep warm. Strain the pan juices and return them to the pan. Degrease. Thicken as desired with beurre manié. Return the chickens to the pan, add the carrots, mushrooms, and thawed peas, and cook slowly about 15 minutes to heat thoroughly. Sprinkle with chopped parsley before serving.
Serves 6 to 8.

FRENCH ROLLS

See Basics, page 181.

BIBB LETTUCE WITH MUSTARD VINAIGRETTE

4 heads Bibb lettuce
½ cup Mustard Vinaigrette (see Basics, page 173)

Wash and dry the lettuce leaves and arrange them on individual chilled salad plates. Drizzle with mustard vinaigrette. Serves 6 to 8.

APPLES AND PEARS JEANNETTE

5   Golden Delicious apples
5   winter pears, quite firm
1   cup sugar
¼   cup butter
1   cup heavy cream

Preheat oven to 425°. Peel and core the apples and pears and slice in thin wedges. Toss together and spread in a flat baking dish, generously buttered. Sprinkle with the sugar and dot with the butter. Bake, uncovered, about 45 minutes, until the sugar has carmelized. Stir every 15 minutes to coat the fruit evenly with the sugar syrup as it forms. When done, remove from the oven and push the fruit away from the edges of the baking dish, pouring a little of the cream in as you go, and stirring the cream into the syrup. Serve warm, passing extra heavy cream if desired. Serves 6 to 8.

Specialties of the House

GREEN AND BLACK OLIVES

SHRIMPS GALORE   RICE RING

LEMON CAKE ROLL

FRENCH OR CALIFORNIA CHABLIS

I named this dish "Shrimps Galore" because they are so tasty you will want to have plenty. The rice ring, accented with green and red peppers and mushrooms is a beautiful accompaniment, filling and delicious. For dessert, impress your guests with a natural after seafood—lemon cake roll.

SHRIMPS GALORE

3   to 5 pounds green shrimp
2   tablespoons oil
½   onion, diced
½   green pepper, diced
¼   cup white wine, or more if needed
    Dash salt

Shell and devein the shrimp. The amount needed will vary according to the size of the shrimp and the size of the appetites of you and your guests. In a large skillet, sauté the onion and pepper in oil. Place a single layer of shrimp on top and sauté 1 minute. Turn and sauté 1 minute more. Remove from pan and start a new batch of shrimp. Repeat this process until all the shrimp are sautéed. Now return all the shrimp to the skillet and add the wine. Cook 6 minutes and salt lightly. The wine should be exhausted. Toss the shrimp to coat with the thick, syrupy sauce in the pan. Serves 6 to 8.

RICE RING

1½   cups long grain rice, uncooked
3   cups water
¾   teaspoon salt
2   tablespoons green pepper, finely diced
2   tablespoons sweet red pepper, finely
     diced, or pimiento, chopped
4   tablespoons fresh mushrooms, sliced
2   tablespoons butter

Bring the water and salt to a rolling boil and pour in the rice gradually so as not to break the boil. Reduce the heat and simmer, covered, 25 minutes, or until all the moisture is absorbed. Meanwhile, melt the butter in a skillet and sauté the green and red pepper until just soft. Add the mushrooms and sauté until the mushrooms are just tender. Do not overcook.

Butter a 6-cup ring mold. Combine the vegetables with the rice and pack the mixture into the mold, compressing as much as possible. Let stand for 3 or 4 minutes and then invert onto a heated serving plate. The center may be filled with some of the shrimp. Serves 6 to 8.

LEMON CAKE ROLL

Sponge Cake Roll (see Basics, page 186)
Lemon Curd (see Basics, page 192)
Powdered sugar

Make the sponge cake roll according to the directions in Basics. Cool the cake thoroughly. Prepare a lemon filling according to the directions given in the recipe for lemon curd in Basics. Unroll cake, spread with filling, and reroll. Sprinkle the top with sifted powdered sugar. Cut on the diagonal for prettier slices. Serves 6 to 8.

A Dinner for Good Friends

CONSOMMÉ

POT AU FEU   VEGETABLE GARNISH

FRENCH BREAD

GREEN SALAD

APRICOT TART

SAINT-EMILION (FRENCH)

This menu is a boon for the hostess who chooses to be unharassed. It's easy to stretch for unexpected guests; simply drop another chicken or one more beef brisket in the pot au feu. This will produce one of the finest consommés you will ever taste. Surround the chicken and beef with vegetables of contrasting color and offer lots of crusty French bread. Then serve green salad with your own house dressing. For an unexpected dessert, try apricot tart. Once considered the food of the gods, apricots still convey a touch of the exotic—especially when they are glazed and sprinkled with pistachios.

CONSOMMÉ

See Basics, page 168, or use the broth from cooking the Pot au Feu, straining and clarifying it according to the directions in Basics.

POT AU FEU

  4 **pounds boneless beef (brisket preferred)**
     Bouquet Garni (see Basics, page 177)
  1 **onion, studded with 4 whole cloves**
  1 **tablespoon salt**
  8 **whole black peppercorns**
  1 **4- to 5-pound stewing chicken**
  2 **tablespoons oil**
  3 **or 4 beef marrow bones**
16 **small whole carrots**
16 **whole white onions**
  3 **to 4 leeks, if available**

Place the beef in a pot with water to cover. Bring to a boil and simmer 5 minutes. Remove the meat from the pot and rinse. Discard the water and wash the scum from the pan. Replace the beef in the pot with fresh water, the bouquet garni, onion, salt, and peppercorns. If desired, beef bouillon cubes or a beef extract may be added to the water to intensify the flavor of the stock. Simmer 1 hour. Meanwhile, brown the chicken whole in the oil in a heavy skillet, turning frequently. Add the chicken and marrow bones to the pot and simmer for another 2 hours or until the beef is tender. Skim foam as needed.

The vegetables can be cooked separately *al dente* or they can be added to the pot to be cooked in the stock if there is room. This latter method adds a great deal of flavor to your stock.

To serve, remove the beef and chicken to a heated platter and keep warm. Strain the broth through a sieve lined with dampened cheesecloth. Skim off fat. (If time permits, refrigerate broth until fat solidifies and remove.) Return to pot and reduce by boiling briskly to intensify flavor. If necessary, clarify with egg whites as described in Basics. This makes a nice first course served in the living room. Slice the beef thinly on the diagonal and arrange on a large platter. Disjoint the chicken and arrange the pieces on the platter with the beef. Arrange the vegetables on the same platter if there is room, or on a separate platter.

This meal is best served buffet style. Be sure to offer a variety of mustards, horseradish, and some sour pickles. A little warm vinaigrette is traditionally served with the beef. Serves 6 to 8.

FRENCH BREAD

See Basics, page 180.

GREEN SALAD

Variety of salad greens
Creamy Vinaigrette (see Basics, page 173)

Wash and dry thoroughly several types of salad greens, such as iceberg lettuce, romaine, and Boston lettuce. Watercress, parsley, chives, chervil, fresh tarragon, cucumbers, or green onions may be added as desired. Do not use radishes or tomatoes.

Break the greens (do not cut) into a cold china or glass bowl which may be rubbed with a peeled and halved garlic clove. At serving time, toss with just enough vinaigrette to moisten all leaves. For a final flourish, you may grind some black pepper on the top.

APRICOT TART

½ recipe Pie Pastry for Fruit Pies (see
    Basics, page 185)
½ cup apricot jam, chopped
 1 16-ounce can apricot halves
    Apricot Glaze (see Basics, page 188)
    Powdered sugar
 1 tablespoon unsalted pistachio
    nuts, chopped

Make the pastry according to the directions in Basics and line a tart shell. Preheat oven to 400°. Line the tart shell with waxed paper and fill with dry navy beans or rice to prevent the pastry from bubbling during baking. Bake for 10 minutes until partly done. Remove beans and waxed paper and return to oven until golden, about 5 minutes. Cool slightly. Cover bottom with the chopped apricot jam and arrange the apricot halves rounded side up, on top of the jam. Paint with apricot glaze. Let set. Before serving, sprinkle with sifted powdered sugar and pistachio nuts. Serves 6 to 8.

New England's Gift

NEW ENGLAND CLAM CHOWDER

PILOT CRACKERS

HARVEST CHICKEN PIE   HOT BISCUITS

PICKLED PEACHES   CRANBERRY JELLY

WATERMELON PICKLES

LEMON SOUFFLÉ PIE

APPLE CIDER

Whether New England made clam chowder famous, or vice versa, here's a version straight from the state of Maine. Serve it with crisp pilot crackers for authenticity. A harvest chicken pie goes well with this. Rich and savory with chicken and vegetables, and topped with small baking powder biscuits, it exemplifies the harvest season. Pickled peaches, cranberry jelly, and watermelon pickles accompany this bounty. For a climax, bring on the lemon soufflé pie!

NEW ENGLAND CLAM CHOWDER

¼ pound salt pork, diced
1 onion, minced
4 potatoes, peeled and cubed
1½ cups water
2 7½-ounce cans minced clams
2 cups milk
    Salt
    White pepper
1 tablespoon butter

In a skillet, cook the salt pork over medium high heat until the fat is rendered and the pork has formed crisp cracklings. Drain and reserve the cracklings. Discard all but 2 tablespoons of the fat and sauté the onion until golden. Transfer to a soup pot and add the potatoes and water. Cook 10 minutes, or until the potatoes are tender. Drain the clams, reserving juice, and add to the chowder. Cook another 10 minutes. Scald the milk, heat the clam juice, and add both to the chowder. Simmer about 20 minutes, seasoning with salt and pepper. Just before serving, stir in the butter and drop the cracklings on top. Serve with crisp pilot crackers. Serves 6 to 8.

HARVEST CHICKEN PIE

1 4- to 5-pound stewing hen
    Bouquet Garni (see Basics, page 177)
1 onion, studded with 4 cloves
    Salt
4 black peppercorns
¼ teaspoon thyme or tarragon
3 potatoes, peeled and diced
4 carrots, peeled and sliced
    Biscuits (see Basics, page 183)
2 recipes Velouté Sauce (see Basics, page 170)

Bring to a boil enough water to cover the chicken and drop in the chicken. Add the bouquet garni, onion, salt, peppercorns and thyme or tarragon; simmer, covered, until the chicken is tender, about 1½ hours. Remove the chicken from the broth and cool slightly. Remove the meat from the bones and cut into small pieces. If you wish to intensify the flavor of the broth, you may return the skin and bones to the pan and cook vigorously, reducing the volume. Strain the broth.

Cook the potatoes and carrots in separate pans of salted water until just tender, or *al dente*.

Preheat oven to 425° and make small biscuits according to the directions in Basics. Bake 12 to 15 minutes and remove from oven. Preheat oven to 350°.

Make a double recipe of velouté sauce, using 1 cup milk and 1 cup of the broth from the chicken. Taste for seasoning. Add the chicken, potatoes, and carrots; pile the mixture into a shallow casserole. Top with a layer of biscuits. Bake the casserole 30 minutes or until thoroughly heated. Pass remaining biscuits and your favorite pickled peaches, cranberry jelly, and watermelon pickles. Serves 6 to 8.

LEMON SOUFFLÉ PIE

1 baked pie shell (see Basics, page 185)
3 eggs
1 cup sugar
¼ teaspoon salt
⅓ cup lemon juice
    Grated rind of 1 lemon

Bake the pie shell according to the directions in Basics. Separate the eggs and lightly beat the yolks. Combine the yolks, ½ cup of the sugar, salt, lemon juice, and rind in the top of a double boiler. Cook for 15 minutes over boiling water, stirring. Cool.

Preheat oven to 400°. Beat egg whites until soft peaks form. Gradually add the remaining ½ cup sugar. Carefully fold the whites into the lemon mixture. Pile into the baked pie shell. Bake for 10 to 12 minutes.

Foreign Specialties

England

HIGH TEA

CHEESE RAREBIT   ENGLISH MUFFINS

POTTED SHRIMP   CUCUMBER SANDWICHES

LEMON CURD TARTS   CHERRY BUMPERS

BRANDY SNAPS   DUNDEE CAKE   ROCKS

TEA   CREAM SHERRY

Nothing is quite as English—or as inviting—as a high tea. Polish your silver; get out a linen tablecloth, your best china, and some cloth napkins (or "serviettes," as the British call them); set a small vase of fresh flowers in the center of the table. To this exquisite setting add all the dishes listed here, both sweet and savory. Finally, rinse out your teapot with a bit of hot water to warm it up and add a heaping teaspoon of tea for each cup to be served. Bring a kettle of water just to the boil, pour it into the pot and allow to steep for 5 minutes. Pop on a tea cozy and you're ready to serve the perfect "cuppa."

CHEESE RAREBIT

2 tablespoons butter
2½ to 3 cups grated cheese (Cheddar, Swiss, or a mixture of both)
1½ cups stale beer
2 teaspoons Worcestershire sauce
2 teaspoons dry mustard
½ teaspoon salt
Dash ground red pepper (cayenne)
2 eggs

In the top of a double boiler or chafing dish, melt the butter over simmering water. Add the cheese gradually, stirring constantly. When the cheese is melted, add the beer, reserving ¼ cup. Stir until smooth. Combine the Worcestershire sauce with the mustard, salt, and red pepper and add to the rarebit. Beat the eggs with the reserved beer. Gradually add about 1 cup of the hot cheese mixture to the beaten eggs and then add this to the rarebit. Stir until it is heated through. Serve over English muffins. Serves 6 to 8.

ENGLISH MUFFINS

See Basics, page 182.

POTTED SHRIMP

1 cup butter
1 teaspoon salt
½ teaspoon nutmeg
Dash ground red pepper (cayenne)
1 pound cooked shrimp, peeled, deveined, and chopped

Clarify ½ cup butter in the following manner. Melt the butter slowly. Remove from heat. Let stand a few minutes to allow the white milk solids to sink to the bottom of the pan. Skim off the clear, yellow butter. Set aside.

Melt the remaining ½ cup butter. Stir in seasonings and shrimp. Heat gently. Pour into small ramekins or straight-sided bowls. Pour the clarified butter over. Chill overnight. Serve as a spread with a fine white bread. Serves 6 to 8.

CUCUMBER SANDWICHES

See "The May Bowle," page 31.

LEMON CURD TARTS

1 recipe Lemon Curd (see Basics, page 192)
1 recipe Pie Pastry for Fruit Pies (see Basics, page 185)

Make the lemon curd and pie pastry according to the directions in Basics. Preheat oven to 400°. Roll out the pastry and cut in rounds to fit at least 8 individual tart pans. Trim edges with a sharp knife. If you have enough tart pans, you can place an empty pan over each tart to prevent bubbling. Otherwise, prick the pastry with the tines of a fork. Bake at 400° for 12 minutes. Remove empty tart pans if used and reduce heat to 350°. Continue baking until the crusts are a pale golden color. Cool completely before filling with the lemon curd. Serves 8 or more, depending on the size of the tart pans.

CHERRY BUMPERS

1 recipe Pie Pastry for Fruit Pies (see Basics, page 185)
1 10-ounce jar cherry preserves
1 egg beaten with 1 tablespoon water

Make pie pastry according to the directions in Basics. Preheat oven to 400°. Roll out the pastry into two 10-inch squares and cut each into four 2½-inch squares. In the center of each square place about 1 teaspoon cherry preserves. Using a pastry brush dipped in water, slightly dampen the edges of each square and fold into a triangle. Press firmly around edges with dampened fingers to seal. With a sharp knife cut a tiny slash in the top of each to release the steam while baking. Brush lightly with the egg and water mixture and place on baking sheets. Bake about 20 minutes or until pastry is done. Makes 32.

BRANDY SNAPS

¾ cup butter
¾ cup sugar
½ cup molasses
 2 teaspoons ginger
1½ cups flour, sifted
¼ teaspoon salt

Preheat oven to 300°. Generously butter a cookie sheet. Melt the butter and add the sugar and molasses. Stir in the ginger. Remove from heat. Add the flour and salt. Drop the batter from a teaspoon onto the buttered cookie sheet, well apart—only 4 to 6 on a sheet. Bake about 12 minutes. Quickly roll hot cookies around the handle of a wooden spoon with the top side of the cookie on the outside. Cool on a rack. These may also be served after dinner with brandy, if desired. Some, it is said, dip the crisp cookie into their brandy. Makes 2 dozen.

DUNDEE CAKE

 1 cup butter
 1 cup sugar
 5 eggs
 2 cups flour, sifted
½ teaspoon salt
 1 cup raisins
⅔ cup currants
⅔ cup sultanas (golden raisins)
⅓ cup candied mixed fruit
    Grated rind of 1 orange
¼ cup flour
¾ teaspoon soda
 1 teaspoon milk

Preheat oven to 275°. Grease an 8x8-inch pan and line it with baking parchment paper. Grease the paper.

Cream the butter with the sugar until light and fluffy. Add the eggs, one at a time, beating well after each. Sift the flour again with the salt and add gradually to the batter, blending well. Combine all of the fruits and the orange rind in a bowl with the ¼ cup flour, tossing to coat each piece of fruit with flour. Stir the fruit into the batter. Mix the soda with the milk and add to the batter, stirring to blend thoroughly. Pour the batter into the prepared pan and bake 2½ to 3 hours, until it tests done with a cake tester. Cool in the pan for 10 minutes; then turn out onto a rack to cool. For ease in slicing and serving, cut the cake into three long, narrow loaves; then slice thinly. Makes 48 (16 slices to a loaf).

ROCKS

1½ cups raisins
1½ cups water
3½ cups flour, sifted
 2 teaspoons baking powder
 1 teaspoon soda
 1 teaspoon salt
½ teaspoon cinnamon
    Dash cloves
 1 cup shortening
1½ cups sugar
 3 eggs
 1 teaspoon vanilla

Preheat oven to 350°. Grease a cookie sheet. In a saucepan, bring the raisins and water to a boil, reduce heat, and simmer gently until all the water is absorbed. Set aside until cool.

Sift dry ingredients together. Cream the shortening with the sugar until light and fluffy. Add the eggs, one at a time, beating well after each. Add the vanilla. By hand, fold in the dry ingredients, mixing well. Fold in the raisins and combine thoroughly.

Drop from a teaspoon onto prepared cookie sheet. Bake about 25 minutes. Remove to a rack to cool. Makes about 7 dozen.

Britain

COCKALEEKIE

VEAL AND HAM PIE

LEAF LETTUCE SALAD WITH BACON DRESSING

**CHOCOLATE STEAMED PUDDING
WITH VANILLA SAUCE**

TEA   GREY RIESLING (CALIFORNIA)

The charmingly named Scottish dish "cockaleekie" heads this typically British menu, ideal for an informal luncheon. As one might surmise, cockaleekie is a soup featuring both chicken and leeks—a redolent, hearty combination born in the Highlands. The veal and ham pie that follows is a particularly flavorful example of the savory meat pastries the British have made a specialty. Follow it with a wilted lettuce salad topped with hot bacon dressing, chocolate "pud" for dessert and, of course, tea. Could anything be better on a brisk winter afternoon?

COCKALEEKIE

1   4- to 5-pound stewing hen, cut up
1   onion studded with 4 cloves
3   ribs celery, including leaves
2   carrots
4   sprigs parsley
2   teaspoons salt
6   whole peppercorns
3   medium leeks
½   cup long grain rice, uncooked

Wash the chicken, removing excess fat. Place in a large kettle and add just enough water to cover. Add all remaining ingredients except the leeks and rice. Bring to boiling, reduce heat, partially cover, and simmer gently until the chicken is tender, about 2 to 3 hours. Remove the chicken and strain the broth through a sieve lined with damp cheesecloth. Skim the fat off the broth. Remove the skin and bones from the chicken and cut the meat into bite-sized pieces. Reserve.

Split the leeks in half lengthwise and wash carefully under cold running water. Cut crosswise into 2-inch lengths, cutting only slightly into the green portion. Bring a small amount of water to boil in a saucepan, add the leeks, and cook just until soft. Drain and reserve.

Measure the broth and if necessary, add more broth or water to make 2 quarts. Heat and add the rice. Simmer until the rice is done, about 20 minutes. Add the chicken pieces and leeks. Heat well and serve. Serves 6 to 8.

VEAL AND HAM PIE

1½   pounds boneless veal, cut in 1-inch cubes
     Bouquet Garni (see Basics, page 177)
1   onion studded with 4 cloves
1½   pounds ham, cut into 1-inch cubes
4   hard-cooked eggs, coarsely diced
     Salt
     Pepper
½   teaspoon marjoram
2   cups Béchamel Sauce (see Basics, page 170)
1½   recipes Pie Pastry (see Basics, page 185)
1   egg beaten with 1 tablespoon water
2   tablespoons dry sherry

Place the veal in a large saucepan, cover with cold water, and bring to a boil. Cook 5 minutes and drain into a strainer. Rinse the meat with cold water and clean the pan. Return the veal to the pan, add the bouquet garni and onion, and cover with cold water. Bring to a boil, reduce heat, and simmer partially covered until the meat is tender, about 1 to 1½ hours. Drain, reserving broth. Return the broth to the pan and boil briskly until it is reduced to about ½ cup. Reserve. Make the béchamel sauce according to the directions in Basics.

Make the pastry according to the directions in Basics. Line a deep 2-quart baking dish with pastry. Roll out additional pastry for the top, cutting it about ¼-inch larger in diameter than the dish. Reserve. Cut decorative flowers and leaves from the pastry scraps to decorate the top. Preheat oven to 425°.

Pile the veal, ham, and hard-cooked eggs into the pastry-lined dish in layers, sprinkling with the salt, pepper, and marjoram. Thin the béchamel sauce with the reserved veal broth and pour it over the filling. Cover with the top and brush with the egg-water mixture. Arrange the decorations on the top crust and brush again with the egg wash. Insert the

round tip from a pastry tube in the center of the top for a steam vent, or use a pastry bird if you have one. Alternatively you may cut slashes in the top. Bake about 45 minutes or until the pastry is cooked and golden and the filling is piping hot. Just before serving, pour the sherry down into the pie.
Serves 6 to 8.

LEAF LETTUCE SALAD WITH BACON DRESSING

5 slices bacon, diced
2 tablespoons water
3 tablespoons vinegar
2 tablespoons sugar
2 bunches leaf lettuce, torn
2 tablespoons parsley, chopped
   Dash salt

Sauté the bacon until crisp. Remove from pan and reserve. To the drippings in the pan, add the water, vinegar, and sugar. Cook until the sugar is dissolved and the flavors blended. Wash and dry the lettuce and tear into a large salad bowl. Sprinkle with salt and pour the hot dressing over. Toss lightly to wilt the lettuce. Just before serving, sprinkle the bacon bits over the top of the salad. Serves 6 to 8.

STEAMED CHOCOLATE PUDDING WITH VANILLA SAUCE

2 cups flour, sifted
2 teaspoons baking powder
½ teaspoon salt
1 cup sugar
2 tablespoons butter
2 eggs
1 cup milk
2 1-ounce squares unsweetened
   chocolate, melted
   Vanilla Sauce (see Basics, page 190)

Prepare a pudding steamer mold, a small bundt pan, or a metal ring mold. The mold must be metal and have a center hole for even cooking. Grease the pan well and the inside of the top. If using a pan that does not have a tight fitting lid, make a double layer of aluminum foil and grease the side that will be placed over the pudding.

Sift the flour, baking powder, and salt together and set aside. Cream the sugar with the butter, add the eggs, and beat well. Add the milk and then stir in the dry ingredients, mixing thoroughly. Blend in the melted chocolate. Fill the mold not more than ⅔ full. Cover tightly.

Place the mold on a trivet in a heavy pan. Pour 3 inches of boiling water around the mold. Cover the pan. bring the water to a boil, reduce heat, and steam the pudding about 2 hours. When done, remove the cover carefully. Let stand in the mold about 10 minutes and then invert onto a serving dish. Serve with vanilla sauce. Leftover pudding may be re-steamed successfully. Steam just until reheated. Serves 6 to 8.

Middle East

MEZZAS

SHISH KABOB   COUSCOUS

MELON RING WITH STRAWBERRIES

TURKISH COFFEE

What a shame that the Middle East, which has so much to offer in the way of delectable and truly inventive menus, is so often ignored by food buffs in the United States. As fine as coq au vin and cassoulet may be, what serious gourmand does not welcome the challenge of a new cuisine with its unfamiliar ingredients and unexpected tastes? Here we have just that. Entice your guests with a dazzling assortment of mezzas and then continue the enchantment with a jewel of Middle Eastern cuisine: lamb shish kabob, skewered and served on a bed of couscous. For dessert, there's a colorful melon ring with strawberries.

MEZZAS

Mezzas are the popular Middle Eastern version of the hors d'oeuvres table, similar to, but uniquely different from, salmagundi or the Italian antipasto. They are served in the same manner, in raviers, or matching serving pieces. They are always accompanied by pita, or pocket bread. Guests fill the pocket of the bread with whatever assortment of mezzas they wish, experimenting with several different combinations. Offered in sufficient quantity, they can certainly stand as a meal in themselves.

Marinated Garbanzos: Drain one 16-ounce can garbanzos (chick-peas). Rinse in cold water, put in small saucepan, add fresh water, and bring to a boil. Drain. Add ¼ cup chopped parsley, ¼ cup chopped onion, ½ teaspoon pressed garlic, 3 tablespoons lemon juice, 2 tablespoons olive oil, ½ teaspoon salt, and a pinch of ground red pepper (cayenne). Mix well to coat each chick-pea. Serve at room temperature.

Eggplant Purée: Wrap a medium-sized eggplant in foil and bake at 350° until tender, about 35 to 45 minutes. Cool slightly and peel. Chop and then mash, adding ¼ cup lemon juice, ¼ cup chopped onion, 1 tablespoon olive oil, 1 tablespoon chopped parsley, 1 large garlic clove, minced, and 1 teaspoon salt. Taste for seasoning. Garnish with pine nuts, chopped parsley, and chopped onion.

Feta Cheese: This is a cheese that is kept in brine. To serve, dry on towel and cut in cubes.

Olives: Use Greek olives if possible. Ripe black olives may be substituted.

Taramasalata: Soak 5 slices of white bread with crusts removed in 1 cup cold water for 5 minutes. Squeeze dry with hands. Blend until smooth in blender or food processor. Add one 2-ounce jar of red caviar or ½ cup tarama (Greek caviar), 1 small onion, cut up, and the juice of 1 lemon. Blend until smooth. Add ½ to ¾ cup olive oil, a little at a time, blending between each addition.

Tabbouleh: Place ½ cup bulgur (fine cracked wheat) in a bowl. Cover with boiling water. Soak 30 minutes and drain in sieve lined with cheesecloth. Squeeze dry. Drop in bowl and add 3 tomatoes, 1 cup parsley, and 1 bunch green onions, including part of the tops, all finely chopped. Add ⅓ cup olive oil, ¼ cup lemon juice, 1 tablespoon chopped mint, and 1 teaspoon salt. Toss to combine well. Chill before serving.

SHISH KABOBS ON A BED OF COUSCOUS

3 pounds lamb shoulder or leg,
   cut in large cubes
½ cup oil
½ cup dry red wine
1 clove garlic, minced
½ bay leaf
½ teaspoon rosemary
1 teaspoon salt
2 onions, cut in wedges
1 pound whole mushrooms, trimmed
1 pint cherry tomatoes
2 or 3 green peppers, cut in 1-inch pieces
1 pound couscous (if unavailable,
   substitute 2 cups cooked white rice)

Combine the oil, wine, and seasonings. Marinate the lamb in this mixture for 2 to 6 hours, turning occasionally. Drain the lamb and pat dry. Arrange on skewers, alternating the lamb with the onion wedges. Place the mushrooms, tomatoes, and green peppers on separate skewers. Do not mix or alternate them to allow for different cooking times. Brush the lamb and vegetables with oil. Broil or grill the lamb to taste. When the meat is almost done, cook the vegetables briefly on the grill until they are just tender.

Prepare the couscous according to package directions. If substituting rice, refer to Basics, page 179.

Warm the dinner plates and make a bed of couscous on each one. Using a fork, slide a few chunks of lamb and then a few vegetables onto the bed of couscous. Serve immediately. Serves 6 to 8.

MELON RING WITH STRAWBERRIES

2 to 3 ripe cantaloupe
1 quart strawberries
2 to 4 tablespoons sugar,
   preferably superfine
1 tablespoon Kirsch or
   orange-flavored liqueur, optional

Early in the day, wash and hull the strawberries. Marinate them in the sugar and Kirsch or liqueur for at least 1 hour before serving. Slice the melons into rings, hollowing out the center. Place a ring on individual chilled plates and pile the strawberries in the center. Serves 6 to 8.

TURKISH COFFEE

For each serving:
1 demitasse cup cold water
1 teaspoon powdered Turkish coffee
1 drop rosewater or
   1 cardamon seed, optional
   Sugar, optional

For desired number of servings, place coffee in a small deep saucepan or Turkish coffee pot and stir in the cold water. Heat to a boil and remove from heat; repeat the heating process 3 times. Add optional ingredients. Serve in demitasse or Turkish coffee cups.

Indonesia

NASI GORENG   SAMBALS

TROPICAL COCONUT ICE CREAM BALLS

TEA

There are times when a dramatic presentation can make the difference between a merely interesting meal and a truly memorable dining experience. Here, with just a little effort and imagination, you can transport your guests to the exotic Indonesian islands of Sumatra and Java. Comb your cupboards for imported plates, colorful runners or place mats, and brass or tin serving dishes and utensils. They will add immeasurably to the authenticity of your *rijsttafel*, the classic Indonesian rice table. (It should be noted that the recipe for nasi goreng has a few modifications that reflect the Dutch influence. Chicken, beef, and fish would be used in Moslem homes.)

There is one elementary rule in eating rijsttafel and that is that one should eat with a spoon and fork. Whereas the uninitiated diner tends to stir up the whole affair into a pudding, the connoisseur samples each condiment, or sambal, separately. He starts off with the rice—nasi goreng—puts it in the middle of his plate, and then surrounds it with the various offerings, developing a skill comparable to that of a professional wine taster. No two experts, however sophisticated, make the same selections in quite the same order. So you really can't go wrong. Wear a sophisticated look and let yourself go!

NASI GORENG

    2 cups long grain rice, uncooked
    2 eggs
    2 tablespoons milk
    1 tablespoon oil
 1½ pounds lean pork, diced
    2 tablespoons oil
    2 onions, thinly sliced
    1 clove garlic, minced
    2 teaspoons paprika
    2 teaspoons java root powder or
       ½ teaspoon grated fresh ginger
  ½ teaspoon cumin
  ½ teaspoon coriander
       Salt
       Pepper
    1 pound shrimp, cooked
  ¼ pound shredded ham
    4 green onions, sliced

Bring 4 cups salted water to a boil and add rice. Reduce heat and cook, covered, 20 to 25 minutes, until all moisture is absorbed.

Beat the eggs lightly with the milk. Heat 1 tablespoon oil in a skillet, preferably nonstick. When a drop of water will dance in the pan, add the eggs all at once, turning and tilting the skillet so that they spread evenly to fill the bottom of the pan. Cook as if they were a large pancake, just until they lose their gloss and are solid but not brown. Remove to a board and cool. Cut into shreds.

Using a large skillet or wok, heat the remaining 2 tablespoons oil until very hot. Add the pork and cook, stirring and tossing until lightly browned and cooked through. Add the sliced onions and cook, stirring until soft. Add the seasonings and mix well. Now add the cooked rice and shrimp, tossing and turning to mix well. Continue cooking until the rice is well heated. Pile onto a heated platter or large flat bowl. Garnish the top with the shredded eggs and ham and the sliced green onions. Place in the center of the buffet or serving table, surrounded by the sambals. Serves 6 to 8.

SAMBALS

Select matching bowls if possible, about the size of soup bowls. Fill them with all or some of the following items, the more the better.

Chopped salted peanuts, skins removed
Chutney—one or more types
Shredded coconut, toasted
Cucumber, peeled, seeded, and sliced
Banana, sliced
French-fried onions (canned acceptable)
Hard-cooked egg yolks, sieved
Hard-cooked egg whites, finely chopped
Mixed pickles or pickle relish

TROPICAL COCONUT ICE CREAM BALLS

    1 quart vanilla ice cream
    2 cups grated coconut
    1 cup grenadine syrup
    1 cup Simple Syrup (see Basics, page 188)
       Juice of 1 lemon

Spread the coconut in a pie pan or similar shallow pan or dish. Slightly soften the ice cream. Using a dipper, form ice cream balls, either 3 small ones or 1 large one per guest. Quickly roll each ball as it is formed in the coconut, set on a chilled pan, and freeze until firm.

Combine the grenadine syrup, simple syrup, and lemon juice. Pass to pour over the ice cream. Lotus bowls make particularly nice serving dishes for this dessert. Whatever dishes you use, it is best to chill them before serving the ice cream in them. Serves 6 to 8.

Greece

LEMON SOUP

SPINACH PIE

GREEK SALAD   GREEK BREAD

FLAN WITH ROSEWATER

WHITE TABLE WINE (CALIFORNIA)

From one of the oldest civilizations on earth comes a meal imbued with tradition yet as modern as tomorrow. We begin with lemon soup, an unlikely sounding dish that will win the enterprising host or hostess kudos for both originality and taste appeal. Essentially a chicken broth with rice, the soup is enriched at the last minute with the Greek lemon-egg sauce *avgolemono*, which adds an unexpected and delightful tang. Proceed to spinach pie *(spanakopita)*—a mouth-watering concoction featuring fresh spinach, feta cheese, and strata of flaky phyllo dough. Competing for attention is a Greek salad, artfully constructed by piling layers of colorful vegetables atop lettuce leaves and dotting them with chunks of feta cheese, ripe olives, and walnut halves. The resulting pyramid is drizzled with a dressing redolent with oregano, lemon juice, and olive oil. This recipe, given to me by a Greek taxi driver, is one of the finest in my foreign collection. Topped off by a rosewater flan, there is only one word for this Hellenic feast: *Eureka*!

LEMON SOUP (SOUPPA AVGOLEMONO)

8 cups Chicken Stock (see Basics, page 168)
½ cup rice, uncooked
4 eggs
3 tablespoons lemon juice
Chopped mint or parsley, optional
Salt
White pepper

Bring the chicken stock to a boil and add rice. Return to boiling, reduce heat, cover, and simmer until rice is cooked, about 15 to 20 minutes.

Beat the eggs. Add the lemon juice slowly, beating constantly. Add a ladleful of the hot soup to the eggs and beat well. Now add the egg mixture to the soup, pouring slowly and whisking briskly. Heat slowly over low heat until the soup thickens. Do not allow the soup to come to a boil because this will cause the eggs to curdle.

Taste for seasoning, adding mint or parsley, salt, and white pepper to taste. You may add more lemon juice if desired. This soup may be served either hot or cold with equal success. Serves 6 to 8.

SPINACH PIE (SPANAKOPITA)

¼ cup olive oil
½ cup chopped onion
¼ cup chopped green onions, including tops
2 pounds spinach, washed and drained, or 2 10-ounce packages frozen spinach, thawed and squeezed dry
2 tablespoons dried dill weed
¼ cup parsley, chopped
½ teaspoon salt
Pepper
⅓ cup milk
4 eggs, slightly beaten
½ pound feta cheese, crumbled
1 cup unsalted butter, melted
1 pound phyllo leaves, thawed

In a large skillet, preferably nonstick, sauté the onions and green onions in olive oil until soft and transparent but not brown. Add the spinach, cover, and cook 5 minutes. Add the dill, parsley, salt, and pepper and cook uncovered, stirring occasionally, until all the liquid is absorbed. Cool. Add the milk, eggs, and cheese, and stir to combine thoroughly. Set aside. Preheat oven to 350°.

To assemble the pie, brush the sides and bottom of a 9x13-inch ovenproof serving dish with melted butter. Unroll the phyllo leaves and cut the stack in half crosswise. Trim about 1 inch off one end to make the leaves about 8½x12½ inches. Cover the phyllo with a damp towel or plastic wrap to keep it from drying out as you work.

Line the bottom of the dish with 2 leaves. Brush the top leaf with melted butter. Repeat this procedure until half the phyllo has been used. Use the phyllo trimmings if necessary to fill in near the edges of the dish. Keep the layers as even as possible. Spread the spinach mixture evenly over the top layer of phyllo. Repeat the process of layering 2 phyllo leaves with melted butter until all the phyllo is used. Brush the top layer generously with melted butter.

Bake until pastry is crisp and golden, about 45 minutes. Let stand 10 minutes before cutting. Serves 6 to 8.

GREEK SALAD

- 2 heads Boston lettuce
- 1 cucumber, sliced
- 1 green pepper,diced
- 8 radishes, sliced
- 6 green onions, sliced
- 3 small tomatoes, sliced
- 12 ½-inch cubes feta cheese
- 12 ripe olives, Greek if possible
- 12 walnut halves
- 5 anchovies
  Greek Dressing (see Basics, page 173)

Wash and dry lettuce, separating leaves; arrange them on a large round plate. Add slices of cucumber, green pepper, radishes, green onions, and tomatoes in layers, making each layer smaller, in pyramid fashion, until all the vegetables are used.

Tuck in the cheese, olives, and walnuts on the sides of the pyramid. Garnish with anchovies. Drizzle Greek dressing over the salad. The dressing will trickle down and marinate the salad. Pass additional dressing if desired. Serves 6 to 8.

GREEK BREAD

Make the French bread dough as directed in Basics, page 180. When it is time to form the loaves, grease 4 pie tins. Divide the dough into 4 equal parts and pat into rounds to fit the pie tins. They should be quite thin. Let rise about 30 to 45 minutes. Preheat oven to 400°.

Combine 1 teaspoon salt with ¼ cup water. Brush the loaves with the salt water and sprinkle with sesame seeds if desired. Bake about 20 to 25 minutes until browned and done. Makes 4 small round loaves.

FLAN WITH ROSEWATER

- ¾ cup sugar
- 3 eggs
- 2 egg yolks
- 2 cups evaporated milk or half-and-half
- ½ cup sugar
- 1 teaspoon vanilla
- ½ teaspoon rosewater

Select a 1-quart charlotte mold, soufflé dish, or ring mold for this dessert. You will need a larger pan that will hold the mold surrounded by hot water for baking. Preheat oven to 375°.

Melt the ¾ cup sugar in a heavy pan until it is golden. Pour into the mold. Set aside.

Beat the eggs and egg yolks until light. Add the evaporated milk or cream, ½ cup sugar, and flavorings. Pour this custard over the caramel in the mold. Set the mold in a larger pan and pour boiling water around it to a depth of about 2 inches. Bake about 40 minutes, or until a cake tester inserted in the center comes out clean. Remove from the pan of water and cool in the mold. Chill. Unmold to serve by loosening the sides with a thin knife. Serves 6 to 8.

Belgium

ENDIVE SALAD

BEEF CARBONNADE   **CARROTS VICHY**

FRENCH BREAD

CHOCOLATE ROLL WITH CHOCOLATE SAUCE

GAMAY BEAUJOLAIS (CALIFORNIA) OR

BROUILLY BEAUJOLAIS (FRENCH)

Ask an American to complete the phrase "Belgian———" and he or she will probably say "waffles." Yet the pride of Belgian cuisine, as well as one of the country's major industries, is endive. Crisp and bitter, this refreshing vegetable is sautéed, stuffed, and braised for use in Belgian soups and attractive side dishes. We show it off here in a tangy vinaigrette, as a prelude to the classic carbonnade—strips of beef flambéed in gin, simmered in beer and beef stock, and sauced to perfection. Accompanied by carrots Vichy, this is a dish that can easily—and thriftily—be stretched to feed a crowd. Complete your menu with a luscious chocolate roll and you have all the makings of a veritable Flemish feast.

ENDIVE SALAD

1   pound (8 to 12) Belgian endives
½ cup parsley, chopped
    Mustard Vinaigrette (see Basics,
    page 175)
    Salt and pepper to taste

Separate the leaves of the endives and wash them carefully under cold running water. Dry in a kitchen towel. Cut the leaves lengthwise into thin julienne strips. Sprinkle with parsley. Just before serving, toss with mustard vinaigrette, salt, and pepper, using just enough dressing to moisten the leaves. Arrange on individual chilled salad plates. Serves 6 to 8.

BEEF CARBONNADE

1   12-ounce can beer
3   pounds lean beef, chuck or round
3   tablespoons oil
½ cup gin
3   cups Beef Stock (see Basics, page 168)
1   onion, sliced
2   sprigs parsley
2   16-ounce cans small whole potatoes
½ pound fresh mushrooms
    Butter
2   tablespoons water
2   tablespoons cornstarch

Several hours before preparing this recipe, open the can of beer so that it will lose its carbonation and become stale.

Slice the beef thinly. (This is more easily done if it is slightly frozen.) Heat the oil in a skillet and sauté the beef a few pieces at a time, transferring them to a large pan or Dutch oven as they brown. When all the beef has been browned, pour the gin over it and light with a kitchen match. When the flames die down, add the beef stock and beer. Sauté the onion in the skillet and add to the beef. Add the parsley sprigs, cover, and simmer or bake in a 350° oven at least 2 hours or until the beef is tender.

Meanwhile, rinse the canned potatoes and place in a pan with fresh water. Bring to a boil; drain immediately. Slice the mushrooms, or leave them whole if they are small. Sauté lightly in butter. About ½ hour before the beef is done, add the potatoes and mushrooms to the pan.

When ready to serve, remove excess grease from the pan. Mix the water with the cornstarch and add slowly to the carbonnade, stirring constantly, using only as much as needed to thicken the sauce to a desirable consistency. Serve with warm French Bread (see Basics, page 180). Serves 6 to 8.

CARROTS VICHY

2   bunches carrots
2   tablespoons butter
1   teaspoon salt
1   teaspoon sugar
    Chopped parsley

Peel the carrots and slice into thin coins. Place in a heavy saucepan with the butter, salt, and sugar. Add enough water to come about halfway up the depth of the carrots. Bring to a brisk boil; cook, uncovered, stirring occasionally, until all liquid is exhausted, about 7 minutes. Sprinkle with chopped parsley to serve. Serves 6 to 8.

FRENCH BREAD

See Basics, page 180.

CHOCOLATE ROLL

6 eggs, separated
  Pinch salt
¾ teaspoon cream of tartar
½ cup cake flour
¼ cup cocoa
¾ cup sugar
1 cup heavy cream
2 tablespoons powdered sugar, sifted
1 teaspoon vanilla
  Chocolate Sauce (see Basics, page 190)

Preheat oven to 375°. Grease a 15½x10½x1-inch jelly roll pan, line it with waxed paper, and grease the paper.

Beat the egg whites with the salt until foamy. Add the cream of tartar and beat until stiff peaks form. Sift the flour and cocoa together and set aside.

Beat the egg yolks with the sugar until lemon colored. Add the dry ingredients, blending well. Gently fold this mixture into the whites. Pour into the prepared pan and spread evenly. Drop the pan onto the counter from a height of about 6 inches to break the air bubbles. Bake about 15 minutes, watching carefully to prevent overbrowning.

Sprinkle the cake with powdered sugar and cover with a towel. Place a board over the pan and then turn the board and pan over, releasing the cake onto the towel-covered board. Gently remove the waxed paper and trim any hard edges. Folding the edge of the towel over the top of the cake, roll up the cake and towel together from the long edge and let cool.

Whip the cream with the powdered sugar and vanilla. Unroll the cooled cake, remove the towel, and spread the cake with the cream. Reroll and place on a long board or serving tray. Chill at least 2 hours. Pass chocolate sauce to accompany the roll. Serves 6 to 8.

Spain

GAZPACHO

PAELLA   BOLILLOS

PINEAPPLE WITH LEMON ICE

ZINFANDEL (CALIFORNIA)

OR WHITE RIOJA (SPANISH)

The glories of Spanish cuisine provide the inspiration for this most refreshing of all summer menus. Neither a soup nor a salad, but the best of both, gazpacho is the perfect way to begin this light but filling meal. My version calls for the raw vegetables to be coarsely chopped, not blended, and then stirred into seasoned tomato juice, chilled, and served in frosty cups topped with a sprig of fresh basil. Proceed to a classic from Valencia: paella, a rich and colorful blend of seafood, chicken, sausages, vegetables, and saffron rice. Pass the pineapple for dessert and your guests will be tempted to shout "*olé!*"

GAZPACHO

4 fresh tomatoes, peeled, seeded,
   and finely chopped
2 cucumbers, peeled, seeded,
   and finely chopped
1 green pepper, finely chopped
1 onion, finely chopped
1 46-ounce can tomato juice
¼ cup olive oil
3 tablespoons wine vinegar
1 clove garlic, minced
¼ cup parsley, chopped
½ teaspoon basil
½ teaspoon salt
¼ teaspoon sugar
¼ teaspoon pepper
   Fresh basil leaves or chopped parsley
   Dry Croutons (see Basics, page 177)

Chop all the vegetables by hand. Do not use a blender or food processor because each vegetable should retain its own unique texture. Combine the vegetables and add the remaining ingredients except for the garnishes. Cover and chill.

To serve, place an ice cube in each chilled glass bowl or cup. Add a leaf of fresh basil or some chopped parsley and ladle in the gazpacho, being careful to distribute a serving of vegetables in each dish. Top with croutons.

An alternate serving method is to chop the vegetables and place each in a separate bowl. Combine the tomato juice with the remaining ingredients except for the garnishes and chill well. Ladle the soup into the chilled glass bowls or cups and let the guests help themselves to the vegetables of their choice. Serves 6 to 8.

PAELLA

2 tablespoons oil
1 medium onion, minced
1 clove garlic, minced
2 cups long grain rice, uncooked
1 green pepper, diced
1 teaspoon salt
   Dash ground red pepper (cayenne)
½ teaspoon saffron
4 cups Chicken Stock (see Basics, page 168)
8 cherrystone clams, thoroughly scrubbed
1 pound medium shrimp, cooked
8 meaty pieces chicken, fried or baked
4 Polish sausages, sliced and sautéed
1 10-ounce package frozen tiny peas,
   thawed
1 2-ounce jar chopped pimiento

Using the traditional paella pan or a large round flameproof baking dish, heat the oil. Add the onion and sauté until soft and transparent. Add the garlic and cook briefly, stirring. Add the rice and sauté, stirring to coat all the rice with the oil. Now add the green pepper, salt, red pepper, saffron, and chicken stock. Bring to a boil, cover, reduce heat, and simmer until the rice is almost cooked, about 15 minutes.

Place the seafood, chicken, and sausages in a random pattern on top of the rice, cover and cook for 10 minutes more. The clams will pop open while cooking. Do not serve any unopened clams. Remove the cover and spoon the peas in a ring around the edge of the paella. Scatter the pimiento over the top. Do not cover after the peas have been added. Cook just a little longer to heat the peas. Serve from the pan. Serves 6 to 8.

BOLILLOS

Make dough according to the directions for French bread in Basics, page 180. After the second rising, divide the dough into 16 equal pieces. Shape each piece into a ball, then roll with hands into a 5-inch oval; pinch ends to form boat shape. As rolls are shaped, place on greased baking sheets. Let rise until double, about 30 minutes. Preheat oven to 400°.

Using a sharp knife, cut a slash 2 inches long and ¾-inch deep lengthwise down the center of each roll. Combine ½ teaspoon cornstarch and ¼ cup water; heat to boiling. Cool slightly and brush on top of each roll. Bake about 20 to 25 minutes until golden brown. Makes 16.

PINEAPPLE WITH LEMON ICE

2 ripe fresh pineapples
1 pint lemon sherbet
2 tablespoons sugar, preferably superfine
1 tablespoon Kirsch
   or orange-flavored liqueur

Leaving the tops intact, cut the pineapples into quarters lengthwise. Using a sharp, thin knife, core and remove the fruit from the shell, reserving the shells. Cut the fruit into cubes, sprinkle with the sugar and Kirsch or liqueur, and chill. Also chill the shells. Working as quickly as possible, make small balls of the sherbet with a melon baller. Place them on a chilled flat pan and freeze until firm. Just before serving, place the shells on individual chilled plates. Pile the fruit and lemon sherbet balls on the shells and serve immediately. Serves 8.

Italy

ANTIPASTO SALAD

CARBONARA   ITALIAN ROUND LOAVES

STROMBOLI IN ERUPTION

RED TABLE WINE (CALIFORNIA) OR

BARDOLINO (ITALIAN)

If there is a more beautiful way to begin a summer meal than with antipasto, I don't know what it is. Indeed, as the renowned Italian cooking teacher Marcella Hazan comments, "Nothing in all gastronomy plays so boldly upon the eye to excite the palate and set gastric juices in motion." Here some of my favorite antipasti are combined for a lovely salad. The second course is bread and carbonara, a rich combination of spaghetti, ham, and Parmesan cheese. The aptly named "Stromboli in eruption" makes a truly spectacular conclusion, especially if children are present.

ANTIPASTO SALAD

1   head romaine lettuce
1   10-ounce package frozen lima beans
½   pound fresh green beans
2   cups zucchini, sliced
1   6-ounce can pitted black olives, drained
2   medium tomatoes, cut in wedges
½   pound Italian salami, cut in cubes
½   pound carrots, cut julienne
1   cup Italian Dressing (see Basics, page 174)

Wash the romaine and break the leaves off the stem, leaving them whole. Cook the lima beans according to package directions, drain, and marinate in some of the Italian dressing. Cook the green beans according to the directions given for green beans with mimosa garnish, page 38, and marinate in Italian dressing. Cook the carrots very briefly in salted water, about 2 minutes, until they are just tender crisp. Drain and marinate in Italian dressing. Place a romaine leaf on each individual salad plate and casually pile some of each of the remaining ingredients on top. Pass additional Italian dressing. Serves 6 to 8.

CARBONARA

1   pound spaghetti
1   pound well-flavored ham, cut in matchsticks
2   tablespoons olive oil
3   eggs, slightly beaten
¼   cup grated Parmesan cheese
½   cup parsley, chopped

Cook the spaghetti according to package directions, being careful not to overcook. Drain and reserve, keeping hot. Meanwhile, sauté the ham in the oil in a large skillet. Add the eggs. Quickly add the hot pasta and stir well to combine. Add the cheese and parsley and serve immediately. Serves 6 to 8.

ITALIAN ROUND LOAVES

See Basics, page 180.

STROMBOLI IN ERUPTION

Hot Milk Sponge Cake (see Basics, page 186)
Pastry Cream (see Basics, page 191)
½   cup Simple Syrup (see Basics, page 188)
2   tablespoons rum or Strega
4   egg whites (reserve eggshells)
¾   cup powdered sugar
Brandy

Preheat oven to 375°. Grease and flour three 8-inch round pans. Make the hot milk sponge cake according to the directions in Basics. Pour into the prepared pans and bake 25 to 30 minutes, until they test done with a cake tester. Cool in the pans 10 minutes; then turn out onto racks.

Make the pastry cream and simple syrup according to the directions in Basics. Add the rum or Strega to the simple syrup. Split each cake layer in half horizontally. Sprinkle each layer with the flavored syrup. Place one layer on a heat-proof cake plate and spread with pastry cream. Repeat until all layers are used, but do not spread pastry cream on the top layer.

Preheat oven to 450°. Just before serving, beat the egg whites until foamy. Gradually add the powdered sugar and continue beating until stiff peaks form. Cover the cake with the meringue and dust with sifted powdered sugar. Set 3 empty eggshell halves on the top of the cake. Bake for about 5 minutes until meringue is golden. Remove from the oven, fill the shells with warm brandy, and ignite at the table. Serve when the flames are exhausted. Serves 8 to 10.

Italy

MELON AND HAM

SALTIMBOCCA   NOODLES

BROILED TOMATOES

ZABAGLIONE OVER COLD POACHED PEARS

CHIANTI (CALIFORNIA OR ITALIAN)

One of the beauties of Italian cuisine is the strongly seasonal character of its dishes. Here is one of the finest summer menus you will ever encounter. Beginning with a delightful appetizer of melon and prosciutto, it progresses to saltimbocca, a Roman contribution which translates literally as "jump into the mouth," served with fresh homemade pasta and broiled tomatoes. Properly presented, this particular combination of foods creates a mosaic on the plate unsurpassed in texture, color, and taste. And to complete a perfect meal, a perfect dessert (and my own personal favorite), zabaglione. This deceptively simple custard of egg yolks, Marsala, and sugar must be prepared precisely according to directions and served at once. Work, to be sure, but mounded over a very cold, lovingly poached pear, it is nothing short of glorious. *Buon gusto!*

MELON AND HAM

1   ripe honeydew melon
8   thin slices prosciutto ham
1   lime
    Pepper in a grinder

Cut the honeydew melon into eight equal lengthwise wedges. Loosen the fruit from the rind with a sharp, thin knife, but leave the rind in place for serving. Setting the wedges rind side down, make a lengthwise cut down the center of the slice, and then make several crosswise cuts to divide the serving into bite-sized pieces, leaving all pieces in place. Cut each slice of prosciutto into narrow strips, roll the strips, and place them between the melon chunks randomly. Place a wedge of lime on each serving plate with the melon and ham, and pass the pepper grinder. Serves 8.

SALTIMBOCCA

3   pounds boneless veal
4   slices prosciutto ham
2   tablespoons butter
2   tablespoons oil
¾   cup Veal or Chicken Stock
    (see Basics, page 168)
½   cup dry white wine
    Dash white pepper
¼   teaspoon oregano

Slice the veal thinly and cut into 32 round scallops, removing all fat and connective tissue. Place the scallops between sheets of waxed paper and pound gently but firmly with a flat mallet until very thin and about 3 inches in diameter. Cut the prosciutto into 16 rounds. Sandwich each slice of ham between 2 slices veal.

Heat the butter and oil in a skillet and sauté the veal sandwiches on both sides, a few at a time, being careful not to crowd the pan. Remove from pan as they are browned.

Secure each scallop with a wooden pick and return to the pan. Add ½ cup stock, the wine, and the seasonings. Bring to a boil, reduce heat, cover, and simmer for about 15 minutes or until the meat tests done when pricked with the tip of a sharp knife.

Remove the veal to a warm platter and keep warm, removing picks. Add the remaining ¼ cup stock to the pan juices and stir to dissolve all particles in the pan. Cook briskly over high heat, reducing the juices in volume about one-half, until they become thick and syrupy. Taste for seasoning. Strain the sauce over the veal and serve. Serves 8.

NOODLES

1   recipe Noodles (see Basics, page 184)
    or 1 pound broad noodles, purchased
2   tablespoons butter
½   pound fresh mushrooms
½   cup butter, softened
1   cup Swiss or Parmesan cheese, grated
    or a combination of both
    Salt
    Pepper
½   cup warmed heavy cream, or more

Cook the noodles in boiling salted water until just tender—do not overcook. Drain. Melt the 2 tablespoons butter in a skillet. Slice the mushrooms and sauté them very briefly, until just tender. Turn the drained noodles into a large heated bowl. Add the softened butter, cheese, and seasonings and toss until the butter has melted and all ingredients are well combined. Toss in the mushrooms. Add enough cream to make a thin sauce. Serve immediately. Serves 6 to 8.

BROILED TOMATOES

See "Breakfast at Brennan's," page 19.

ZABAGLIONE OVER COLD POACHED PEARS

8 top quality canned pear halves, drained
½ cup pear juice
¼ cup sugar
¼ cup water
1 teaspoon vanilla
5 egg yolks
½ cup sugar
½ cup sweet Marsala

Make a syrup of the pear juice, ¼ cup sugar, water, and vanilla. Add the pears and poach about 10 minutes. Chill in the syrup. Just before serving, drain the pears and place one half in each serving dish. Top with the zabaglione sauce.

To make the sauce, beat the egg yolks with a whisk in the top of a double boiler over simmering water. Beating continuously, add the sugar and then the Marsala. Cook and beat until the mixture swells into a thick soft mass, about 12 minutes. Be careful that the simmering water does not touch the bottom of the pan in which the sauce is being cooked, because this will cause the eggs to cook too fast and become scrambled. Serve immediately. Serves 8.

Hungary

LIPTAUER CHEESE WITH VEGETABLE GARNISH

WHOLE GRAIN BREAD

BEEF GOULASH   DUMPLINGS

NUT RODITIES

MOUNTAIN RED (CALIFORNIA)

OR EGRI BIKAVÉR (HUNGARIAN)

After France and Italy, there is probably no country in Europe with as rich or varied a culinary tradition as Hungary. Influenced by its neighbors—Austria, Czechoslovakia, Yugoslavia, and Russia—Hungary has taken a *mélange* of languages and flavors and emerged with its own complex, very distinctive cuisine. How ironic, then, that so many American cooks consider the noble Hungarian *gulyas* a humble, rather bland dish, suitable perhaps for one's family but never for company! Carefully prepared and well seasoned with sweet Hungarian paprika, goulash can easily hold its own alongside boeuf bourguignonne. And what accompaniments! Fluffy white dumplings, preceded by the incomparable Liptauer cheese garnished with vegetables and seasonings. And for dessert, a confection every bit as mouth-watering as real Hungarian strudel but requiring only about one-tenth as much time to prepare. The secret? Greek phyllo dough. Well, if the Hungarians can borrow from other cuisines, so can we!

LIPTAUER CHEESE

6   ounces cream cheese
½   cup small curd cottage cheese
2   ounces Camembert cheese
1   tablespoon Parmesan cheese
1   large, loose-leafed iceberg lettuce
    Vegetable garnishes (recipe follows)

Combine the cheeses and mix well. Wash the lettuce, removing any discolored outer leaves. With a stainless steel knife, remove enough of the center to form a cavity big enough to hold the cheese mixture. Fill the cavity with the cheese and chill. Place the lettuce in a shallow bowl for support when serving.

Place the Liptauer cheese on a buffet table together with plenty of whole grain bread and the garnishes. Guests can then help themselves, spreading the cheese mixture on a bread slice and topping it with the garnishes of their choice. Serves 6 to 8.

GARNISHES FOR LIPTAUER CHEESE

Using a separate small jar or pot for each, provide any assortment of the following garnishes:

Chopped parsley
Capers
Red caviar
Chopped green onions or chives
Chopped ripe olives
Chopped dill
Sharp Dijon-style mustard
Caraway seeds

Also have on the table a salt shaker, pepper mill, paprika shaker, and a pot of whipped butter.

WHOLE GRAIN BREAD

See Basics, page 181.

BEEF GOULASH

3   pounds beef round
¼   cup oil
3   medium onions, thinly sliced
1   clove garlic, minced
2   teaspoons sweet Hungarian paprika
1   teaspoon vinegar
1   teaspoon salt
    Freshly ground black pepper
1   teaspoon caraway seeds
½   teaspoon marjoram
1   cup dry red wine
½   cup Beef Stock (see Basics, page 168)
    Beurre Manié (see Basics, page 171)
1   cup sour cream
    Dumplings (recipe follows)

Cut the beef into 1-inch cubes and dry them with paper toweling. In a heavy casserole, brown the beef, a few pieces at a time, in the oil. Remove the cubes as they brown. and reserve. Add the onions to the pan in which the beef was browned and cook, stirring, over low heat until transparent. Add the garlic and cook briefly. Moisten the paprika in the vinegar and add to the onions, cooking and stirring about 2 minutes. Return the meat to the casserole and add the seasonings, the wine, and beef stock. Bring to a boil and cover. Reduce the heat and simmer, or place in a 325° oven, until the beef is tender, about 2 hours. Add more stock if necessary. When the meat is done, remove any excess grease from the goulash and thicken as desired with beurre manié.

Ladle the goulash onto a serving platter and surround with dumplings. Spoon a dollop of sour cream on top and pass additional sour cream. Serves 6 to 8.

DUMPLINGS

2 cups flour
1 teaspoon salt
3 teaspoons baking powder
2 tablespoons shortening
1 cup milk

Combine the dry ingredients. Cut in the shortening with a pastry blender or 2 forks. Add the milk and work just enough to combine.

Grease a shallow pan, such as a layer cake pan, that can fit into a larger pan on a trivet. Or, if you have one, grease the rack of a steamer. Drop the dumplings from a spoon onto the greased surface, place on the trivet and pour boiling water in the bottom of the larger pan. Cover, bring water back to the boil, reduce the heat, and steam the dumplings for 15 minutes. Do not uncover while steaming. This method of cooking gives the dumplings a unique texture that cannot be duplicated through boiling. Serves 6 to 8.

NUT RODITIES

1 cup Simple Syrup (see Basics, page 188)
1 cinnamon stick
   Juice of ½ lemon
¼ cup honey
2 cups assorted nuts, finely chopped
   (walnuts, pecans, almonds, pistachios)
1 teaspoon cinnamon
¼ teaspoon ground cloves
½ cup sugar
1 pound phyllo leaves, thawed
1 cup butter, melted

Make the simple syrup according to the directions in Basics, but cook it with the cinnamon stick, lemon juice, and honey. Simmer about 3 minutes. Cool.

Preheat oven to 300°. Butter a 15½x10x1-inch jelly roll pan.

Unroll the phyllo leaves and remove 2 sheets. Keep remaining dough covered with a damp towel or plastic wrap as you work, to prevent drying out. Brush the 2 sheets of dough with melted butter. Spread 4 to 5 tablespoons of the nut mixture over the dough to within 1 inch of the edge. Starting at the long edge, roll up as for a jelly roll. Repeat until all the nut mixture has been used.

Place the rolls close together on the buttered pan. Brush the tops with more melted butter. Cut diagonally into 2-inch pieces, leaving the rolls formed. Bake until crisp and golden, about 30 minutes. Remove from oven. While still hot, dip each piece into the cold syrup. Drain on a rack. Makes about 20.

Russia

ZAKOUSKI VODKA

KULEBYAKA SOUR CREAM DILL SAUCE

CHERRIES FLAMBÉ

RUSSIAN TEA

SPARKLING RED (CALIFORNIA) OR

CHAMPAGNE (RUSSIAN)

What hors d'oeuvres are to the French and antipasto is to the Italians, zakouski—literally "small bites"—are to the Russians. As simple or as lavish as you wish, they are a perfect prelude to kulebyaka, a classic of Russian cuisine. An elegant, flaky pastry loaf, we have simplified its preparation here by substituting the more American ground beef for the traditional salmon filling. Topped with a silken sour cream sauce flavored with dill, the results are every bit as tempting and much easier on the budget. With regal cherries flambé as the finale, this is a meal worthy of a czar.

ZAKOUSKI

Zakouski are the Russian version of salma-gundi and are served in the same manner. Use *raviers* or attractive small serving dishes and fill with the items listed below. Pass plenty of buttered slices of small dark rye bread.

Buttered Radishes, Cucumbers in Sour Cream Sauce, Pickled Beets, and Pickled Mushrooms: See "Eating In or Out of Doors," page 58.

Dill Pickles: Use your favorite brand of pickles.

Herring: Use a good quality pickled herring.

Pâté: Purchase a good brand of pâté de foie gras, chill at least 2 hours, and slice thinly.

Stuffed Eggs: Cook 6 eggs in boiling water about 12 minutes, rolling gently with a wooden spoon the first 5 minutes to center the yolks. Remove immediately to a pan of cold water. Peel under cold running water. Slice in half lengthwise and remove the yolks. Mash the yolks with a fork and blend in just enough mayonnaise to moisten. Add ¼ teaspoon dry mustard, or to taste, and a dash of salt. Place the yolk mixture in a pastry bag fitted with the star tip and pipe into the whites. Sprinkle with paprika.

KULEBYAKA

    1   recipe Pie Pastry (see Basics, page 185;
        reduce shortening to ¾ cup)
    ½   cup shortening
    1   medium onion, chopped
    2   tablespoons oil
  1½   pounds lean ground beef
    1   teaspoon salt
    ¼   teaspoon pepper
    ¼   teaspoon marjoram
    ¼   teaspoon thyme
    ½   cup Brown Sauce (see Basics, page 170)
    3   hard-cooked eggs, chopped
    1   egg beaten with 1 teaspoon water
        Sour Cream Dill Sauce (recipe follows)

Make the pastry according to the directions in Basics, reducing the amount of shortening as indicated above. Roll out in a rectangle and dab with an additional ¼ cup shortening. Fold in half and roll out again, dabbing with the remaining ¼ cup shortening. Fold again and roll. Fold and wrap in a towel; chill in the refrigerator while making the filling.

Sauté the onion in the oil until transparent. Add the ground beef and sauté until browned but not dry. Drain the grease from the pan. Add the seasonings and brown sauce. Cool and stir in the chopped hard-cooked eggs. Preheat oven to 425°.

Roll the dough out into a 10x14-inch rectangle. Spread with the filling and roll as for a jelly roll. Place seam side down on a baking sheet and brush with the egg wash. Make leaf cutouts with dough trimmings and decorate the top of the roll. Brush again with the egg wash. Bake 10 minutes at 425°, then reduce heat to 375° and bake 35 to 45 minutes more, until browned. Serve with sour cream dill sauce. Serves 6 to 8.

SOUR CREAM DILL SAUCE

    1   tablespoon butter
    3   tablespoons dill weed
    1   tablespoon flour
    1   cup Beef Stock (see Basics, page 168)
        Juice of ½ lemon
        Dash salt
        Pinch sugar
    ½   cup sour cream

Melt the butter in a small, heavy saucepan and add the dill. Sauté briefly; then stir in the flour to make a roux. Add the stock all at once and cook, stirring until smooth and thickened. Season with the lemon juice, salt, and sugar. When heated through, remove from heat and carefully fold in the sour cream.

CHERRIES FLAMBÉ

    1 1-pound can pitted black cherries
    ¼ cup sugar
    ¼ cup lemon juice
    ¼ cup orange juice
    ¼ cup brandy
    1 quart vanilla ice cream

Drain the cherries and combine the cherry juice with the sugar. Marinate the cherries in the sweetened juice for 15 minutes.

When ready to serve, bring your chafing dish to the table and light it. Pour the cherry juice and sugar into the pan and heat until the sugar is dissolved and the juice is warm. Add the cherries and heat, basting often. Pour the lemon and orange juice over the fruit and stir gently to combine. Warm the brandy in a small pan over a candle and pour it over the cherries. Ignite carefully with a fireplace match. When the flame is exhausted, spoon the cherries and some of the juice over individual dishes of vanilla ice cream.

Other fruits such as peaches or apricots may be substituted for the cherries.
Serves 6 to 8.

RUSSIAN TEA

In a teapot, place 4 whole cloves, ¼ teaspoon grated orange rind, and a small piece of bay leaf. Add 3 tablespoons tea and 6 cups boiling water. Steep 5 minutes for a strong black tea. Strain into teacups and pass strawberry or ginger jam or orange marmalade to sweeten. Serves 8.

Russia

BLINIS AND CAVIAR

CHICKEN CUTLET

HOLLANDAISE-BÉCHAMEL SAUCE

KASHA

CUCUMBER SALAD

PASHKA   KULICH

CHAMPAGNE (CALIFORNIA OR RUSSIAN)

Nowhere in the world was Easter as glorious a celebration as in Russia. This year, why not welcome spring to your home with this incomparable Easter menu? From blinis (bite-size buckwheat pancakes) and caviar through the fabulous Russian Easter creations pashka and kulich, it is a triumph of tradition and taste. Pashka, by the way, is not one of those desserts you whip up at the last minute, but I guarantee that this richest, most luscious cheesecake of all is worth every minute you spend on its preparation. Customarily molded in a pyramid shape, it is garnished with candied fruit and nuts forming the Cyrillic initials *XB*—Christ is risen. Accompany it with slices of kulich, a tall, cylindrical coffee cake which Russian women took to midnight mass on Easter to be blessed by the priest. Blessed or not, it is something else.

BLINIS AND CAVIAR

1   **cup buckwheat pancake mix**
1   **cup buttermilk**
1   **egg, separated**
1   **tablespoon oil**
3   **hard-cooked eggs**
½   **cup green onions, chopped**
½   **cup sour cream**
2   **or more 2-ounce jars lumpfish caviar**

Combine the pancake mix, buttermilk, and egg yolk and chill at least 1 hour. Beat the egg white until stiff peaks form and fold into the pancake batter. Heat the oil on a griddle and make dollar-sized pancakes. They may be wrapped in foil and frozen. To serve, thaw and heat in the oven in foil.

Serve the blinis hot on a warming tray.

Separate the hard-cooked eggs and chop the whites. Sieve the yolks. Put yolks and whites in separate dishes. Put the onions and sour cream in matching dishes. Place the opened jars of caviar in a bowl of chopped ice and surround with the other garnish dishes.

Guests place a little caviar on a blini and top with the garnishes, as they desire. They usually take 3 at a time, putting them on little plates and eating them with their fingers. Serves 6 to 8.

CHICKEN CUTLET

8   **slices white bread, crusts removed**
½   **cup milk**
1   **2½- to 3-pound broiler-fryer chicken**
2   **whole chicken breasts**
1   **egg**
1½   **teaspoons salt**
     White pepper
1   **egg, beaten**
1   **cup sifted bread crumbs**
2   **tablespoons oil**
2   **tablespoons butter**
½   **cup Chicken Stock (see Basics,**
     page 168)
     Hollandaise-Béchamel Sauce (recipe
     follows)

Tear the bread and soak in the milk. Remove the skin and bones from the chicken and chicken breasts. Force through a meat grinder twice or process in a food processor until well ground. Put in a bowl and work in the soaked bread, egg, salt, and pepper. Shape into cutlets resembling pork chops, not too thick. Dip the cutlets in the beaten egg and coat with bread crumbs.

Heat the oil and butter in a heavy skillet and fry the cutlets until golden, a few at a time, not overcrowding the pan. Add more oil and butter as necessary. Transfer to a jelly roll pan. At this point the cutlets may be held until 20 minutes before serving. Preheat oven to 350°.

Add the chicken stock to the pan. Bake 20 minutes or until the cutlets feel firm to the touch. Serve with hollandaise-béchamel sauce. Serves 6 to 8.

HOLLANDAISE-BÉCHAMEL SAUCE

½   **cup Béchamel Sauce (see Basics,**
     page 170)
1   **cup Hollandaise Sauce (see Basics,**
     page 172)

Make the béchamel sauce according to the directions in Basics. It may be made ahead of time and reheated carefully shortly before serving. Make the hollandaise sauce according to the directions in Basics. This must be done at the last minute. Carefully fold the hollandaise sauce into the hot béchamel sauce and combine thoroughly. Pass to serve.

KASHA

1½ cups kasha or long grain rice, uncooked
 1 medium onion, chopped
 3 tablespoons oil
 1 teaspoon salt
⅛ teaspoon pepper
 1 clove garlic on a toothpick
½ stick cinnamon
 3 cardamon seeds crushed
 5 whole cloves
 3 cups Chicken Stock (see Basics, page 168)

Preheat oven to 350°. Place the kasha in a dry skillet and toast over medium heat until lightly browned. Place in a 2-quart casserole. Heat the oil in the skillet and sauté the onion until transparent but not brown. Add to the kasha. Add all remaining ingredients and bring to a boil. Cover and bake about 35 minutes, or until all the liquid is absorbed. Remove from the oven and toss lightly with 2 forks to release the steam. Remove the garlic, cinnamon stick, and cloves before serving. Serves 6 to 8.

CUCUMBER SALAD

 2 cucumbers
¾ cup yogurt
 1 teaspoon salt
 2 green onions, chopped
 1 tablespoon sugar
 1 teaspoon dill weed
    Fresh dill sprigs

Peel the cucumbers. Cut in half lengthwise and remove seeds with a sharp spoon. Slice into crescents. Dry on paper toweling. Chill. Combine the yogurt with the seasonings and onions. Just before serving, toss the cucumbers in the sauce. Pile lightly on individual salad plates and top with a sprig of fresh dill. Serves 6 to 8.

PASHKA

 1 pound dry cottage cheese
¼ pound unsalted butter, softened
 3 ounces cream cheese, softened
 3 egg yolks
¾ cup sugar
½ cup heavy cream
 1 teaspoon vanilla
¼ cup candied pineapple, finely chopped
¼ cup candied cherries, finely chopped
¼ cup sultanas (golden raisins)

Blend the cottage cheese and butter together in a blender or a food processor. Add the cream cheese and process until smooth. In a small bowl, beat the egg yolks. Add the sugar and beat well. Add to the cheese mixture, together with the cream. Blend well. Remove to a bowl and fold in the vanilla and fruit.

Line the traditional pashka mold or a sieve with 2 layers of cheesecloth that has been dampened and squeezed dry. Pack the cheese mixture into the lined mold or sieve and place over a bowl. Place in the refrigerator to drain overnight. Unmold and slice to serve with the kulich. Serves 6 to 8.

KULICH

1½ packages dry yeast
⅓ cup warm milk (105° to 115°)
2 eggs
2 egg yolks
¼ cup sugar
½ teaspoon salt
1¼ cups cake flour
1¼ cups all-purpose flour
½ cup melted butter
¼ cup finely chopped mixed candied fruits: cherries, pineapple, raisins
½ cup powdered sugar
Red food coloring

Dissolve the yeast in the warm milk, adding a few grains of sugar. Beat the eggs and egg yolks until light. Add the sugar and salt and beat well. Add the yeast and stir well. Now add the two flours and the melted butter. Combine thoroughly. Place in a well-greased bowl, cover with a towel, and let rise until light, about 45 minutes to an hour. Punch down and let rise again, about 30 to 45 minutes. Working quickly and lightly, stir in the chopped fruit.

Preheat oven to 400°. Grease well a 1-pound coffee can. To insure the proper shape, do not substitute another size can. Fill only ⅔ full, and shape another small loaf with the leftover dough. Place the dough in the can and let rise until light, about 30 to 45 minutes. Bake about 20 minutes, until golden. Unmold carefully and let cool on a rack. This is a very delicate bread and must be handled with care.

When cool, combine the powdered sugar with just enough water to make a slightly runny consistency. Color to a light pink with a few drops of red food coloring. Pour over the top of the bread and let it drip down the sides unevenly. Serves 6 to 8.

Basics

Stocks and Consommé

QUICK AND EASY STOCK

There are many excellent beef and chicken soup bases marketed commercially in the form of canned broth, bouillon cubes, granules, and pastes. All are fat-free and make fine stock. Follow package directions to substitute them for beef or chicken stock in the recipes given in this book. Keep in mind however, that these broths may be more highly spiced and salty than homemade ones, so season your sauces accordingly. I regularly use B-V Broth and Sauce Concentrate as a substitute for beef stock and bottled clam juice as a substitute for fish stock.

Homemade stocks are easy and fun to make if time is not a factor. Basic stock recipes are included for those who want to start from scratch.

CHICKEN OR VEAL STOCK

4 pounds chicken or veal, meat and bones
3 quarts water
1 onion, sliced
1 tablespoon salt
6 whole peppercorns

Preheat oven to 400°. Place meat and bones in roasting pan. Roast until meat is lightly browned, about 45 minutes. Transfer to soup kettle and add remaining ingredients. Heat to boiling and skim off foam. Reduce heat and simmer 3 to 4 hours. Strain through a large sieve that has been lined with dampened cheesecloth. Allow broth to cool; remove fat. Stock is now ready to use. Makes about 2 quarts.

BEEF STOCK

4 pounds beef, meat and bone
3 quarts water
1 onion, chopped
3 carrots, sliced
1 turnip, sliced
3 sprigs parsley
5 whole cloves
1 tablespoon salt
8 whole peppercorns
1 bay leaf
2 ribs celery, cut up

Preheat oven to 400°. Place meat and bones in roasting pan. Roast until meat is well browned, about 30 to 40 minutes. Transfer to a soup kettle and add remaining ingredients. Heat to boiling and skim off foam. Reduce heat and simmer 3 to 4 hours, skimming as needed. Strain through a large sieve that has been lined with dampened cheesecloth. Allow broth to cool and remove fat. Stock is now ready to use. Makes about 2 quarts.

CONSOMMÉ

The most elegant soup with which to begin a fine dinner. Refer to the index for consommé recipes featuring special garnishes.

Consommé is a clarified stock that has been refined beyond straining. To clarify stock for consommé, add 2 slightly beaten egg whites to each quart of strained stock. Bring slowly to a boil, stirring constantly with a wire whisk. Boil for 2 minutes without stirring. Remove from heat. Let sediment settle to the bottom of the saucepan. Dip clarified stock from the pan and strain through a cheesecloth-lined sieve.

COURT BOUILLON

A seasoned broth for poaching fish.

- 1 **quart water**
- 2 **teaspoons salt**
- 1 **stalk celery**
- 2 **sprigs parsley**
- ⅓ **cup vinegar, lemon juice, or dry white wine**
- ⅓ **cup bottled clam juice**
- 1 **teaspoon pickling spice**
- 1 **onion, sliced**

Combine ingredients and simmer for 20 minutes before adding fish. If desired, strain before using. Place fish, whole or in filets, in a stainless steel or enameled pan. Pour bouillon over to cover the fish. If more liquid is needed, add water. Bring to a boil, reduce heat, and simmer gently until the fish flakes when pierced with a fork, about 8 to 12 minutes for filets, depending on thickness. Check frequently to avoid overcooking. Makes enough for 4 to 5 pounds of fish.

Sauces

BÉCHAMEL SAUCE

A white sauce of medium consistency which is used as a base for hundreds of sauces. You may use it as is for creamed vegetables. Add seafood, chicken, or other leftovers for a fine creamed filling for pastry shells, crêpes, and toast points.

- 1 **cup milk**
- 2 **tablespoons butter**
- ½ **small onion, minced**
- 2 **tablespoons flour**
- ½ **teaspoon salt**
- ⅛ **teaspoon white pepper**
- ⅛ **teaspoon nutmeg**

Heat milk. Melt butter and sauté onion until transparent. Stir in flour. Cook and stir over low heat 2 minutes. Do not let brown. Gradually stir in milk. Heat to boiling, stirring constantly. Strain and transfer to double boiler. Stir in salt, white pepper, and nutmeg. Cook about 5 minutes. Thin with choice of liquids, if desired. Correct seasoning, if necessary. Makes about 1 cup.

VELOUTÉ SAUCE

Replace all or part of the milk in béchamel sauce (see Basics recipe above) with an appropriate white stock (fish, chicken, or veal). Serve whenever you desire a more specific or intense flavor than béchamel sauce provides.

MORNAY SAUCE

This is particularly good when combined with or served over seafood. It also makes a fine topping for vegetables.

- 1 **cup Béchamel Sauce (see Basics recipe above)**
- ¼ **teaspoon dry mustard**
- ½ **to ¾ cup grated cheese (Swiss or a mixture of Swiss and Parmesan) Dash Tabasco or ground red pepper (cayenne), optional**

Add mustard, cheese and optional pepper flavoring to béchamel sauce. Stir to melt the cheese. Do not let boil after adding the cheese. Makes about 1¼ cups.

SAUCE SUPRÊME

A much richer sauce than béchamel.

- 2 **egg yolks**
- ½ **cup cream**
- 1 **cup Béchamel or Velouté Sauce (see Basics recipe above)**

With a fork, mix the egg yolks with the cream in a saucepan. Before putting the pan on the heat, add the hot béchamel sauce gradually to the egg and cream mixture, whisking constantly. Heat gradually, whisking, but do not boil. Makes about 1½ cups.

BROWN SAUCE

A useful sauce to have on hand. Add to any pan drippings to make a wonderful gravy.

- 1½ **tablespoons butter**
- 1½ **tablespoons flour**
- 2 **cups Beef Stock (see Basics, page 168)**

Melt butter. Add flour and whisk until flour starts to turn color. Add stock, whisking. Bring to a boil, reduce heat, and simmer for 20 minutes. Makes about 2 cups.

MUSHROOM SAUCE

Add 1 cup or more sliced, sautéed mushrooms to brown sauce (see Basics recipe above). Serve over sautéed meat.

MADEIRA SAUCE

Add about 2 tablespoons dry Madeira to brown sauce or mushroom sauce (see Basics recipes above). It provides a unique high flavor for beef.

GREEN PEPPERCORN SAUCE

Fresh peppercorns impart a mild pepper flavor to Madeira or brown sauce (see Basics recipes above). You can find them, bottled in water, in gourmet shops. Avoid green peppercorns bottled in vinegar. Add about ¼ cup drained, to the sauce.

SAUCE OF THE WINE MERCHANT

A fine, richly flavored sauce that can dress up any meat or egg dish, and it can turn the lowly hamburger into a kingly entrée.

      ½ cup or more red wine
      1 tablespoon shallots, chopped
      1 bay leaf
      5 sprigs parsley
      2 whole cloves
      5 peppercorns
      2 whole allspice
      1 slice garlic
         Pinch thyme
      1 cup Beef Stock (see Basics, page 168)
         Beurre Manié (see Basics, recipe
         following)
         Parsley, chopped

To the red wine, add shallots, bay leaf, parsley sprigs, cloves, peppercorns, allspice, garlic, and thyme. Boil until reduced one half

in volume. Add beef stock and simmer for 15 minutes. Taste for seasoning and strain. Thicken as desired with beurre manié. Add chopped parsley before serving. Makes about 1 cup.

THICKENERS FOR SAUCES

Although sauces are usually thickened with a roux, there are times when you want to thicken pan juices quickly. At other times you may want to adjust the thickening of a sauce or stew. There are several methods you can use.

CORNSTARCH

Cornstarch adds a translucency to a sauce. One tablespoon of cornstarch will thicken 2 cups or less of liquid. Mix the cornstarch with a little cold water before adding it to the hot liquid. To avoid thinning the sauce, do not overbeat after adding the cornstarch. A sauce thickened with cornstarch should not be reheated.

BEURRE MANIÉ

Beurre manié is extremely helpful in the event a sauce or stew needs some slight adjusting in thickness at the end of cooking. With your fingers, knead equal amounts of flour and butter together. Drop small balls of the kneaded mixture into the hot sauce, one at a time, whisking constantly, until the mixture reaches the desired consistency. For convenience, you can combine a larger quantity in the food processor and keep it on hand in the refrigerator or freezer.

REDUCTION

Reduction is a cooking method used to thicken sauces and intensify their flavor. The liquid is rapidly cooked over high heat and reduced usually to about one half the original volume. Reduced sauces can be used as is or, if desired, thickened further with beurre manié.

HOLLANDAISE SAUCE

The secret of success here is to be careful to add the hot butter very slowly so that complete emulsification can take place. This sauce can be held over hot water for a short time but is difficult to reheat without curdling. For best results, make it as close to serving time as possible.

> 3　egg yolks
> 1½　tablespoons lemon juice
> 　　Dash ground red pepper (cayenne)
> 　　Dash salt
> ½　cup butter

In a blender or a food processor, place egg yolks, lemon juice, red pepper, and salt. Turn on and off quickly, just to blend. Heat the butter until it is hot and bubbling. Turn machine on to high and add the hot butter slowly in a thin stream until the mixture thickens and all the butter has been incorporated. Makes about 1 cup.

MOUSSELINE SAUCE

Add ½ cup heavy cream, whipped, to hollandaise sauce (see Basics recipe above). Serve over poultry, seafood, or any vegetable. The addition of whipped cream lightens the sauce and softens the flavor.

BÉARNAISE SAUCE

This fine, zesty sauce requires the same care in preparing and holding as hollandaise sauce. It makes a wonderful accompaniment to a grilled or sautéed filet mignon.

> ¼　cup dry white wine
> ¼　cup wine vinegar
> 1　tablespoon shallots, chopped
> 1　sprig parsley
> 2　teaspoons tarragon
> 2　peppercorns, crushed
> 3　egg yolks
> ½　cup butter

Combine the wine, wine vinegar, shallots, parsley, tarragon, and peppercorns in a small saucepan. Cook until the liquid has reduced to about 2 tablespoons. Cool slightly. Strain and pour into a blender or food processor. Add egg yolks. Turn on and off quickly, just to blend. Heat the butter until it is hot and bubbling. Turn the machine on high and add the hot butter slowly in a thin stream, until the mixture thickens and all the butter is incorporated. Makes about 1 cup.

CHORON SAUCE

By hand, add a tomato flavoring (2 to 4 tablespoons tomato sauce, purée, or catsup) to the finished béarnaise sauce (see Basics recipe above). Serve as a change of pace from hollandaise.

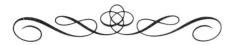

Salad Dressings and Chilled Sauces

VINAIGRETTE SAUCE

Keep this basic dressing on hand at all times. Not only does it turn the simplest of greens into an elegant salad, but it is also used as a marinade for many vegetables. It can be gently heated and served over cooked green vegetables for a zesty addition to the meal.

- ⅓ cup white wine vinegar
- 1 teaspoon salt
- 1 green onion, chopped, or
  1 tablespoon chives, snipped
- 2 sprigs parsley, minced
- ½ teaspoon tarragon
- ½ teaspoon dry mustard
- 1 cup salad oil or a combination of salad and olive oil

Place the vinegar, salt, onion, parsley, tarragon, and mustard in a blender or food processor. Add the oil in a thin, steady stream while blending. (This dressing may be made by hand in a glass pitcher but a machine makes a thicker, tastier dressing.) Makes about 1½ cups.

VINAIGRETTE DELUXE

A colorful dressing with lots of texture.

- 1 tablespoon pimiento, chopped
- 2 tablespoons green onions, minced
- 2 tablespoons parsley, minced
- 2 tablespoons pickle relish
- 1 or 2 hard-cooked eggs, chopped
- ¼ cup carrot, finely grated
- 1⅓ cups Vinaigrette Sauce (see Basics recipe above)

Mix gently by hand. Makes about 2 cups.

MUSTARD VINAIGRETTE

Add 2 tablespoons or more Dijon mustard to vinaigrette sauce (see Basics recipe above). It produces a distinctive flavor change that is particularly appropriate for simple green salads.

CREAMY VINAIGRETTE

For extra richness, add one whole egg to vinaigrette sauce (see Basics recipe above) during the final blending process. For a more pungent dressing, add a few drops of Worcestershire sauce and ¼ teaspoon curry powder.

GREEK DRESSING

The Greek version of vinaigrette features lemon and oregano.

- ¼ to ½ cup red wine vinegar
- ½ teaspoon salt
- 2 tablespoons lemon juice
- ½ teaspoon oregano
  Freshly ground pepper
- 1 cup olive oil or a combination of olive and salad oil

Place the vinegar, salt, lemon juice, oregano, and pepper in a blender or food processor. Add oil in a thin stream to blend. Makes about 1½ cups.

ITALIAN DRESSING

The Italians use garlic as well as oregano to produce their distinctively flavored dressing.

  1 **clove garlic**
  1 **cup olive oil or combination of olive and salad oil**
  ¼ to ½ **cup red wine vinegar**
  1 **teaspoon salt**
  ½ **teaspoon oregano**
    Freshly cracked pepper

Drop a clove of garlic into the oil and let stand for 24 hours. Remove garlic. Place the wine vinegar, salt, oregano, and pepper in a blender or food processor. Blend, adding oil in a thin stream. Makes about 1½ cups.

HONEY FRENCH DRESSING

A subtle dressing to be used with simple greens and fruits.

  ⅓ **cup lemon juice**
  ¾ **teaspoon salt**
  1 **tablespoon sugar**
  ¼ **cup honey**
  1 **cup salad oil**

Mix the lemon juice and salt in a blender or food processor. Add sugar and honey. Slowly add oil, blending constantly. Makes about 1½ cups.

POPPY SEED DRESSING

A more pungent dressing than honey French dressing that can stand up to more strongly flavored fruits and salads.

  ⅓ **cup vinegar**
  ¼ **cup sugar or honey**
  2 **tablespoons apricot jam**
  1 **small onion, minced**
  1 **teaspoon salt**
  1 **teaspoon dry mustard**
  1 **tablespoon paprika, optional**
  1 **cup oil**
  2 **tablespoons poppy seed or celery seed**

Place the first 6 ingredients and paprika, if desired, in a blender or food processor. Add oil, drop by drop at first, then in a steady stream until throughly blended. Add celery or poppy seeds by hand. Makes 2 cups.

MAYONNAISE

If you've never made your own mayonnaise, you're in for a treat. It is deceptively easy to do, as long as you are careful not to add the oil too quickly.

  2 **tablespoons white wine vinegar**
  ¾ **teaspoon salt**
  1 **teaspoon dry mustard**
  1 **whole egg**
  1 **cup salad oil**

Place the vinegar, salt, mustard, and egg in a blender or food processor. Blend for a few seconds. Add the salad oil, drop by drop at first and then in a steady stream. Blend well. Makes about 1⅓ cups.

EMELINE DRESSING

This delicate dressing is one of my favorites, and so I gave it my middle name.

  1 **cucumber, partially pared**
  ½ **cup Vinaigrette Sauce (see Basics, page 173)**
  1 **cup Mayonnaise (see Basics recipe above)**
  1 **teaspoon Dijon mustard**
  ½ **teaspoon tarragon**
  ½ **cup sour cream**
  2 **tablespoons parsley, chopped**

Slice the cucumber in half lengthwise; scoop out seeds. Cut into chunks and place in a blender or food processor. Add vinaigrette sauce and blend. Add mayonnaise, mustard, tarragon, and sour cream. Blend for 2 seconds. Mix in chopped parsley by hand. Makes about 3 cups.

MUSTARD MAYONNAISE

To make a wonderful sandwich canapé spread or a zesty topping for hard-cooked eggs, add 1 tablespoon or more Dijon mustard to 1 cup mayonnaise (see Basics, page 174).

CURRY MAYONNAISE

Add ¼ teaspoon or more curry powder to 1 cup mayonnaise (see Basics, page 174). The curry produces a tangy sauce for hard-cooked eggs or a dip for vegetables.

MAYONNAISE VERTE

The herbs give this mayonnaise a lovely green tint and a delightfully fresh flavor. It is a perfect accompaniment to all cold seafood, especially salmon, and can be used as a dip for vegetables.

- 1 cup Mayonnaise (see Basics, page 174)
- 2 tablespoons chives, snipped
- 2 tablespoons parsley, snipped
- 2 tablespoons watercress, snipped
- 1 tablespoon tarragon

Prepare mayonnaise as directed, except substitute lemon juice for vinegar and add the herbs with the mustard and egg. Cover and chill. Makes a little more than 1 cup.

RUSSIAN DRESSING

This highly flavored dressing doubles as a great dip for vegetables.

- ½ cup Mayonnaise (see Basics, page 174)
- ½ cup chili sauce
- ½ cup sour cream, optional
- ¼ teaspoon salt
- 1 teaspoon Worcestershire sauce
- 1 teaspoon horseradish
- 1 teaspoon onion, grated

Mix well; cover and chill. Makes 1½ cups.

RÉMOULADE SAUCE

Use this lively, textured sauce with cold seafood, hard-cooked eggs, and as a vegetable dip.

- 1 cup Mayonnaise (see Basics, page 174)
- ½ tablespoon Dijon or other sharp mustard
- ¼ cup pickle, chopped
- ½ teaspoon parsley, chopped
- ½ teaspoon tarragon
- ½ teaspoon chives, snipped
- 1 tablespoon capers, chopped, optional
- ½ teaspoon garlic, chopped, optional

Mix additional ingredients into mayonnaise by hand. Cover and chill to blend flavors. Makes about 1¼ cups.

AÏOLI SAUCE

Pungent with garlic, this sauce is made for fish—hot or cold!

- 5 cloves garlic, minced
- 1 egg yolk
- 2 tablespoons olive oil
- 1 cup Mayonnaise (see Basics, page 174)

Place the garlic and egg yolk in a blender or food processor. Blend. Add olive oil and blend. Add the mayonnaise and blend 2 seconds to mix. Makes about 1¼ cups.

INDIENNE SAUCE

Use this sweet-spicy sauce with chicken salad or plain cold chicken, on hard-cooked eggs, and as a vegetable dip.

    1 **cup Mayonnaise (see Basics, page 174)**
    ¼ **cup chutney**
    1 **teaspoon curry powder**
    2 **teaspoons lemon juice**

Mix well; cover and chill. Makes about 1¼ cups.

GREEN GODDESS DRESSING

This classic sauce serves equally well as a salad dressing and as a vegetable dip.

    8 **anchovy filets**
    2 **green onions with tops**
    4 **sprigs parsley**
    ½ **teaspoon tarragon**
    1 **teaspoon chives**
    2 **tablespoons white wine vinegar**
    2 **cups Mayonnaise (see Basics, page 174)**

Place the anchovies, green onions, parsley, tarragon, chives, and vinegar in a blender or food processor. Blend until smooth. Add the mayonnaise, blending briefly to mix. Makes about 2 cups.

SOUR CREAM SAUCE

A delicate sauce to be used over sliced cucumbers and as an accompaniment to my chicken salad.

    1 **cup sour cream**
    2 **tablespoons sugar**
    2 **tablespoons white wine vinegar**
    ½ **teaspoon salt**
    1 **tablespoon Mayonnaise (see Basics, page 174)**

Mix well by hand. Cover and chill. Makes about 1 cup.

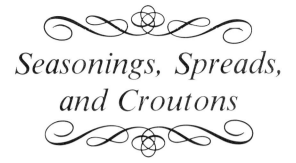

Seasonings, Spreads, and Croutons

BOUQUET GARNI

A bouquet garni is added to soup, court bouillon, and braising kettles, frequently in combination with an onion studded with 4 to 6 cloves. Both are discarded after 2 hours, but the flavor is left behind in the broth.

- 1 carrot, peeled
- 1 rib celery
- 1 bay leaf
- 2 sprigs parsley

Place carrot in celery rib. Place bay leaf and parsley against it and tie securely with cotton string.

HERBES DE PROVENCE

A mixture of the favorite herbs of the South of France—used to flavor sauces and meat and vegetables.

- 2 teaspoons marjoram
- 2 teaspoons basil
- 2 teaspoons thyme
- ½ teaspoon fennel
- 3 bay leaves, crushed
- ½ teaspoon lavender, if available
- 2 teaspoons parsley, dried

Mix gently, cover, and store in a dry place.

SPICE PARISIENNE

This peppery mixture is a wonderful flavoring for pâtés and meat loaves.

- ½ teaspoon cloves
- 2 teaspoons white pepper
- 1 teaspoon black pepper
- 1 teaspoon allspice
- 1 teaspoon nutmeg

Mix gently, cover, and store in a dry place.

HERB BUTTER

Use on grilled burgers and steaks and as a spread for toast.

- ¼ pound butter (1 stick)
- 2 teaspoons chives, snipped
- ¼ teaspoon tarragon
  Parsley, chopped

Soften butter. Add seasonings and mix well.

HERB CHEESE

Try on melba toast.

- 3 ounces cream cheese
- ¼ teaspoon chervil, crushed
- ¼ teaspoon chives, snipped
- ¼ teaspoon parsley, chopped
  Minced garlic, optional

Soften the cheese. Add seasonings and mix well.

CROUTONS

Dry croutons: Preheat oven to 375°. Remove the crusts from firm white bread. Cut into cubes and spread on an ungreased cookie sheet. Bake in oven until golden brown, stirring occasionally.

Buttered croutons: Proceed as for dry croutons. When the croutons are dry and golden brown, remove from oven. Melt enough butter to coat all the croutons in a large skillet. Add the croutons and toss until coated.

Large buttered croutons: Remove the crusts from firm white bread. Cut into large rounds, using a 7-ounce tuna can, top and bottom removed. Butter both sides. Sauté in an ungreased skillet over medium heat until golden brown on both sides.

Marinades

Marinades are used to tenderize meats before broiling or roasting and to impart special flavorings. Always use a glass, stainless steel, or enamel dish, or place the meat in a plastic bag, add the marinade and close. The bag is then placed in a bowl and turned frequently.

MARINADE FOR BEEF

- 1 cup dry red wine
- 1 onion, sliced
- 1 teaspoon salt
- 6 to 8 peppercorns
- 1 clove garlic, minced

Combine ingredients well. Pour over beef and marinate, refrigerated, for at least 6 hours, turning occasionally. Makes enough for up to 5 pounds of meat.

MARINADE FOR LAMB

Prepare marinade for beef, adding 1 teaspoon rosemary.

LEMON MARINADE FOR CHICKEN

- ½ cup oil
- ½ cup lemon juice
- ½ onion, grated
- ½ teaspoon pepper
- ½ teaspoon tarragon
- 1 clove garlic, minced, optional

Mix well, pour over chicken and marinate, refrigerated, for at least 2 hours, turning occasionally. Makes enough for one 2½- to 3-pound chicken, cut up.

CHINESE STYLE MARINADE

- 1 cup soy sauce
- ¼ cup dry white wine or lemon juice
- 1 onion, chopped
- 1 teaspoon grated fresh ginger or ¼ teaspoon dry ginger

Combine ingredients well. Pour over beef, pork, or poultry and marinate, refrigerated, for at least 2 hours. Makes enough for up to 5 pounds of meat or one 2½- to 3-pound chicken, cut up.

Rice

RICE

2½ cups water or stock
1 cup long grain rice
1 teaspoon salt, or less if using stock
1 tablespoon butter

Bring liquid to a boil. Stir in the rice, salt, and butter. Reduce heat, cover, and simmer for 20 minutes. Remove from heat and let stand, covered, until all the water is absorbed. Makes 3 to 4 cups cooked rice.

RICE PILAF

To complete nearly any menu, you can hardly go wrong with rice pilaf. Easy to prepare, it uses ingredients that, once stocked, are nearly always on hand. And its flavors blend well with almost anything.

1½ tablespoons oil
1 cup long grain rice, uncooked
1 small onion, minced
2 cups boiling Chicken Stock (see Basics, page 168)
1 clove garlic on a toothpick
1 stick cinnamon
1 blade star anise, optional
1 teaspoon salt or less, depending on the saltiness of the stock
2 tablespoons butter

Sauté the onion and rice in oil until they are well coated and the color of the rice changes to a milky white. Put into a casserole; add spices and stock. Cover and bake at 350° or cook on top of the stove over low heat for 25 minutes. Remove garlic and toss rice with 2 forks to expel steam. Fold in butter just before serving. Makes 3 to 4 cups.

VARIATIONS OF RICE PILAF

Just before serving, fold in one of the following:

¼ cup pine nuts, toasted
¼ cup almonds, lightly toasted
½ cup or more crisp Chinese noodles

Doughs and Batters

BREADS

Make a habit of beginning your bread baking by proving the yeast. That is, add a few grains of sugar to the yeast as you dissolve it in warm water. If the yeast does not dissolve and begin to bubble after a few minutes, either the water is too hot or too cold, or the yeast is old. Start again with fresh yeast.

FRENCH BREAD

To achieve the lovely crust of high quality French bread, we use three special methods in an attempt to duplicate a baker's oven in the home. First, purchase enough 6-inch square quarry tiles to fit your oven rack. Place the tiles on the rack and preheat them for about 10 to 15 minutes so that they are the same hot temperature as the air in the oven. Place your bread pans on the tiles. Second, on the lower oven rack or on the floor of the oven, place a pan of water. This will add humidity to the oven. Third, mist the bread with water at least 2 times during the early baking period. Use a very, very fine mist for this (a perfume atomizer or plant mister works well).

1½	packages dry yeast
¼	cup warm water (105° to 115°)
1	tablespoon sugar
2	teaspoons salt
1	tablespoon oil
1¼	cups warm water
½	cup warm milk
5	cups all-purpose or unbleached bread flour (variable)
	Cornmeal

Dissolve the yeast in ¼ cup warm water, adding a few grains of sugar. In a large bowl, combine sugar, salt, oil, water, and milk. Add the dissolved yeast mixture. Add flour, 1 cup at a time, mixing well to form a soft dough. It may not be necessary to use all the flour. Knead on a floured board, about 8 to 10 minutes, until smooth and elastic.

Place in an oiled bowl. Cover with a cloth and let rise in a warm place until double in size, about 1 hour or more. Punch down and remove to a lightly floured board.

Divide dough into 3 or 4 parts. Flatten with your hands into an oval. Roll jelly roll fashion into a French bread shape, sealing the ends well by pinching with your fingers. Place seam-side down on cookie sheets that have been sprinkled lightly with cornmeal. Place the loaves far enough apart to allow room for them to rise. Cover with a cloth; let rise in a warm place until almost double in size. Place tiles and pan of water in oven and preheat to 400°.

With a razor blade or very sharp knife, make 3 diagonal cuts across the top of the loaves. This will allow for the even expansion of the bread in the oven. Brush the tops of the bread with lightly salted water (½ cup water and ½ teaspoon salt). Place the cookie sheets on the preheated tiles and bake 25 to 30 minutes or until the bread is lightly browned and done, misting the loaves at least twice during the first 15 minutes of baking time. Cool on rack.

FRENCH BREAD DOUGH (FOOD PROCESSOR STYLE)

¾	package dry yeast
¼	cup warm water (105° to 115°)
2½	cups all-purpose or unbleached bread flour
1	heaping tablespoon dry milk powder
1½	teaspoons sugar
1	teaspoon salt
1½	teaspoons oil
¾	cup warm water

Dissolve the yeast in warm water, adding a few grains of sugar. Set aside. Place the flour, dry milk powder, sugar, salt, and oil in the bowl of the food processor. Blend 2 seconds. Add the yeast mixture. Blend 2 seconds. While the machine is operating, pour the water down the feed tube all at once. Process a few seconds or until the dough forms a ball on the blades. Turn out on a lightly floured board and knead for 4 to 5 minutes. Proceed as for regular French bread. Makes 1 large or 2 small loaves.

FRENCH ROLLS

Use the French bread recipe given on page 180. After the first rising, work 1 unbeaten egg white into the dough with your hands. Form into 2 dozen round rolls. Proceed as for French bread, but bake for 15 to 20 minutes.

ITALIAN ROUND LOAVES

Use the French bread recipe given on page 180. Form the loaves into 3 round, slightly flattened loaves. Place in greased metal pie tins, and bake as for French bread.

PIZZA CRUST

Use French bread dough (see Basics recipe, page 180). Let rise once and punch down. Place in a greased 15½x10½x1-inch jelly roll pan or two greased pizza pans. Flatten with your hands, stretching and flattening the dough to fit the size of the pans. Form an edge around the sides of the pan. Cover and let rise for 10 to 15 minutes. Preheat oven to 425°. Brush with olive oil and use your favorite sauce and cheeses. Bake on the lower oven rack for 20 minutes. You will have an especially crisp crust if you use preheated quarry tiles in your oven, as suggested for French bread.

WHOLE GRAIN BREAD

2	packages dry yeast
1¼	cups warm water (105° to 115°)
½	teaspoon brown sugar
1	egg yolk, beaten
1	cup hot milk
1½	teaspoons salt
3	tablespoons molasses
3	tablespoons honey
5	tablespoons shortening
2	tablespoons orange juice
2½	cups all-purpose or unbleached bread flour
4	cups whole wheat flour
¼	teaspoon ground cumin
1	egg white combined with 4 tablespoons water
	Cornmeal

Combine the yeast with the warm water and brown sugar and stir until dissolved and bubbly. Add the egg yolk. In another bowl, combine the hot milk, salt, molasses, honey, and shortening. Cool until lukewarm and combine with the orange juice and yeast mixture. Add 1½ cups of all-purpose flour and 2 cups of the whole wheat along with the cumin. Beat 1 minute. Mix in the remaining flour to make a stiff dough.

Turn onto a lightly floured board and knead until smooth and elastic, about 8 to 10 minutes. Place in a greased bowl, cover with a cloth, and let rise in a warm place until double in size. Punch down and let rise again for about 30 minutes.

Divide the dough into four parts and shape into round loaves. Place on cookie sheets that have been sprinkled lightly with cornmeal. Let rise for 15 minutes. Meanwhile, place quarry tiles in oven and preheat to 400°.

Slash the loaf tops 3 times with a sharp knife or razor blade. Brush tops with egg white and water mixture. Place cookie sheets on preheated tiles. Bake at 400° for 15 minutes and mist at least twice. Reduce heat to 375° and bake about 30 minutes more.

BASIC ROLL DOUGH

This basic dough may also be used for cinnamon rolls, coffee cake, stollen, and many other holiday breads simply by varying the shape of the loaf and adding desired fillings.

    1½ packages dry yeast
    ¼ cup warm water (105° to 115°)
    2 eggs
    1 teaspoon salt
    ¼ cup sugar
    ⅓ cup oil
    ½ cup warm milk
    3 cups all-purpose or unbleached
       bread flour (variable)

Dissolve the yeast in warm water, adding a few grains of sugar. In a large bowl, beat eggs lightly; add the salt, sugar, oil, and milk. Add the yeast mixture and mix well. Stir in the flour gradually to form a medium soft dough. Turn onto a floured board and knead for about 8 to 10 minutes until smooth and elastic. Place in a greased bowl and let rise in a warm place until double in size. Form into rolls. Cover with a cloth and let rise again until almost double in size, about 30 to 45 minutes.

Preheat oven to 400°. Bake rolls 15 to 20 minutes or until done. Makes 2 to 3 dozen rolls.

CHEESE BREAD

    1½ packages dry yeast
    ¼ cup warm water (105° to 115°)
    2 eggs
    2 teaspoons salt
    ¼ cup sugar
    ½ cup oil
    ½ cup warm water
    ½ cup evaporated milk
    3½ cups all-purpose flour
    1 cup grated medium sharp cheddar cheese

Dissolve the yeast in the ¼ cup warm water, adding a few grains of sugar. In a large bowl, beat the eggs and add the salt, sugar, oil, ½ cup warm water and the evaporated milk. Mix well and add the yeast mixture and 2 cups of the flour. Beat well. Stir in the remaining flour and mix well. Cover, put in a warm place, and let rise until double in size. Beat slightly with a wooden spoon and stir in the grated cheese. Let rise again until almost double.

Preheat oven to 400°. Grease well 4 small loaf pans. Place the dough in the pans and let rise until almost double. Bake in the middle of the oven for 15 to 20 minutes or until golden. If a higher color is desired, a few drops of yellow food coloring and/or some paprika may be added to the dough.

ENGLISH MUFFINS

    1½ packages dry yeast
    ¼ cup warm water (105° to 115°)
    1 egg
    1 cup warm water
    3 tablespoons oil
    1 tablespoon sugar
    2 teaspoons salt
    2 cups all-purpose or unbleached
       bread flour, sifted
    ⅓ cup dry milk powder
    2 cups all-purpose flour or unbleached
       bread flour (variable), unsifted

Dissolve the yeast in the ¼ cup warm water, adding a few grains of sugar. In a large bowl, beat the egg. Mix in the 1 cup water and the oil, sugar, salt, and dissolved yeast. Add 2 cups of the sifted flour and dry milk, beating thoroughly. Stir in enough of the rest of the flour to make a very soft dough and mix well. Cover with a cloth and let rise in a warm place until double. Punch down and let rest for 10 minutes.

Dust a board with cornmeal. Roll the dough out on the cornmeal-covered board to about 1 inch thick. Cut into large rounds, using a 3-inch biscuit cutter. Sprinkle the tops of the muffins with cornmeal. Scraps from the cutting have to be handled very carefully. Press pieces together to avoid incorporating the cornmeal into the dough. Cover with a cloth and let rise until very light, about 30 to 45 minutes.

Preheat an ungreased iron skillet or heavy griddle to medium hot. Cook the muffins for about 15 minutes, turning often. Cool. Split into halves with 2 forks and toast under the broiler. Makes about 8 muffins.

BISCUITS

Cut in 1½- to 2-inch rounds, these biscuits make a fine topping for a meat pie. Cut them in 3-inch rounds for real strawberry shortcake. Add ¾ cup grated cheese for cheese biscuits and herbs of your choice to serve with fowl.

    2 cups flour, sifted
    3 teaspoons baking powder
    2 teaspoons sugar
    ½ teaspoon salt
    ⅓ cup shortening
    ¾ cup milk

Preheat oven to 425°. Grease 2 pie tins. Combine the flour, baking powder, sugar, and salt. Cut in the shortening with 2 forks or a pastry cutter. Add the milk, mixing lightly. Turn onto a lightly floured board and roll about 1 inch thick. Fold half the dough over the other half and roll again lightly. Cut with a 2-inch biscuit cutter and place, touching, in pie tins. Bake about 20 minutes or until lightly golden. These biscuits may be served right from the baking pans. Makes 16.

CORNBREAD

For variety, add ½ teaspoon cumin seeds, ¼ teaspoon ground cloves, and ½ teaspoon cinnamon.

    1 cup flour, sifted
    1 cup cornmeal
    3 teaspoons baking powder
    ½ teaspoon salt
    1 cup milk
    3 tablespoons oil
    2 eggs

Preheat oven to 425°. Generously grease a 7x11-inch cake pan or tiny muffin pans. Blend dry ingredients well. Combine milk, oil, and eggs. Add liquid mixture to dry ingredients and mix thoroughly. Bake 20 to 25 minutes. If tiny muffin pans are used, toss the hot muffins in melted butter before serving. Makes 24 muffins.

POPOVERS

The following recipe will make 5 popovers baked in 5-ounce Pyrex cups. If doubling the recipe, be sure to blend or process in two separate batches.

    3 eggs
    ¾ cup milk
    1 cup flour, sifted
    ¼ teaspoon salt

Blend all ingredients in a blender or food processor until smooth. Pour batter into 5 well-greased 5-ounce Pyrex cups. Put in a cold oven. Set temperature at 400° and bake for 45 minutes.

NOODLES

1½ to 2 cups all-purpose or unbleached
     bread flour
½   teaspoon salt
2   eggs
¼   cup water
1   tablespoon oil

In a large bowl, combine 1½ cups flour and the salt. With a wooden spoon, work in the eggs, water, and oil. Work in additional flour to make a firm dough. Knead slightly and let rest for about 30 minutes, covered. Roll out as thin as possible and cut on a floured board by hand or with a noodle machine. Dry on racks or on board before using. To cook, drop into boiling salted water. If noodles are made on day of cooking, they will be done in 2 to 3 minutes. Test for doneness constantly after 2 minutes. Makes about 4 cups cooked noodles.

FOOD PROCESSOR NOODLES

1¾ cups all-purpose or unbleached
     bread flour
½   teaspoon salt
1   teaspoon oil
2   eggs
2   tablespoons water

Process flour, salt, oil, and eggs for 5 seconds. With motor running, pour water slowly down the feed tube and process until the dough forms a ball. Dough should not be sticky. Turn dough out onto a lightly floured board and knead for a few minutes until it is smooth and elastic. Roll, cut, dry, and cook as in preceding recipe. Makes 4 cups cooked noodles.

SPINACH NOODLES

These fresh, green noodles are wonderful when you want to add color to a plate. They go well with any flavor and may be substituted for plain egg noodles in any recipe calling for them. Drain and squeeze ½ cup cooked, minced spinach to remove as much moisture as possible and add to either of the noodle doughs. Depending on the dampness of the spinach, the water in the noodle recipe may be omitted.

CHOUX PASTE

This is the basic dough for cream puffs and éclairs. You can make tiny puffs for hors d'oeuvres or larger ones for desserts and entrées. Or drop from a teaspoon into a deep fat fryer to produce the delectable French beignets; top with sifted powdered sugar and apricot sauce. Unfilled puffs or éclairs freeze beautifully.

1   cup hot water
½   teaspoon salt
6   tablespoons oil
1   cup plus 2 tablespoons flour
4   eggs

Bring water and salt to a boil. Add oil; bring to a boil again. Add the flour all at once, stirring until the dough forms a ball and leaves the side of the pan. Cool slightly. Turn dough into a large mixing bowl. Add 1 egg at a time, beating very well after each addition. Chill for at least 1 hour.

Preheat oven to 425°. Grease cookie sheets well. Force dough through the plain tip of a pastry bag into 2¼-inch rounds onto sheets for cream puffs. For éclairs, force dough into 3-inch lengths on sheets. Bake 15 minutes, reduce heat to 350°, and bake for 20 minutes or longer, depending on size. Makes about 12 large puffs (3 inches in diameter) or 14 éclairs.

DESSERT CRÊPES

A food with a thousand uses, crêpes can be dressed with almost any sauce or filling. Make them when you have time, stack and wrap tightly in foil, and freeze for a busy day.

      3 eggs
    1½ cups water
      1 cup flour, sifted
     ¼ cup sugar
     ¼ teaspoon salt
      2 tablespoons butter, melted
      1 teaspoon vanilla or 1 tablespoon rum,
          brandy, or other liqueur
          Butter to cook the crêpes

Blend eggs, water, flour, sugar, and salt in a blender or food processor until thoroughly blended. Strain and chill for at least 1 hour. Remove and add the melted butter and flavoring to suit.

Before cooking, have ready by the stove: a 5-inch crêpe pan, small ladle, small spatula to turn the crêpes, and a clean dish towel to stack the crêpes on after cooking. Heat the pan over a medium hot burner and film with butter. Ladle a small amount (a scant 2 tablespoons) of crêpe batter into the hot pan and immediately tilt and turn the pan so that the batter spreads over the entire bottom. Pour any excess batter back into the batter bowl. Cook the crêpe until the top uncooked side turns dull and the underside is lightly browned. Turn the crêpe and lightly brown the underside. Remove from the pan and place to cool on the dish towel. Refrigerate or freeze. Roll in jelly roll fashion or fold handkerchief-style to serve. Makes about 30 dessert crêpes.

ENTRÉE CRÊPES

Omit sugar and substitute chicken stock for the water. Cook in a 7-inch crêpe pan and use about 2½ tablespoons batter per crêpe. Makes about 20 entrée crêpes.

PIE PASTRY

      2 cups flour, sifted
      1 teaspoon salt
     ½ teaspoon baking powder
      1 cup shortening
      6 to 8 tablespoons ice water

Mix dry ingredients well. Cut in the shortening with a pastry blender just until the pieces of shortening are about the size of large peas. Do not overmix. Sprinkle the water over the dough while cutting through the dough with a knife. Add only enough water for the dough to hold together. Shape into a ball, wrap in wax paper, and chill for at least 30 minutes.

Cut the dough in half. Roll out each half on a floured pastry cloth, using a stockinette-covered rolling pin. Always roll lightly and quickly, from the center out to the sides. Fold the dough over the rolling pin and turn into a metal pie pan, taking care not to stretch the dough. This recipe makes one double crust or two baked shells.

To prepare a baked pie shell, place an empty pie pan on top of the crust in the pan. It is not necessary to prick the crust. Bake at 400° for 12 minutes. Remove the empty pan; reduce heat to 350° and bake until crust is a pale golden color.

PIE PASTRY FOR HORS D'OEUVRES

Add ½ teaspoon paprika and either ¼ teaspoon curry powder or ½ teaspoon dry mustard to the dry ingredients for pie pastry (see Basics recipe above).

PIE PASTRY FOR FRUIT PIES

Add 1 tablespoon sugar to the dry ingredients for pie pastry (see Basics recipe above).

HOT MILK SPONGE CAKE

A delicious basic cake recipe. Moist and versatile, it can be used almost any way you like—with any frosting or topping, with or without ice cream and/or sauces.

     1½ cups all-purpose flour, sifted
     ½ teaspoon salt
     3 teaspoons baking powder
     3 eggs
     1½ cups sugar
     1½ tablespoons butter
     ¾ cup hot milk
     1½ teaspoons vanilla

Preheat oven to 375°. Grease three 8-inch round pans and dust with flour. Sift flour, salt, and baking powder together and set aside. Beat eggs and add sugar gradually. Beat for 3 minutes until the mixture ribbons. Sift dry ingredients over eggs and sugar mixture. Fold in gently and quickly. Melt butter in hot milk. Add milk and butter and vanilla to batter and combine quickly. Pour into prepared pans and bake about 25 to 30 minutes or until layers test done with a cake tester.

YELLOW CAKE

This simple, quickly made cake has a rich, buttery, old-fashioned flavor. It is especially good with chocolate frosting.

     2 cups less 2 tablespoons cake flour, sifted
     2 teaspoons baking powder
     ½ teaspoon salt
     ½ cup butter
     1 cup sugar
     ½ teaspoon vanilla
     2 eggs
     ⅔ cup milk

Preheat oven to 375°. Grease two 8-inch round pans or one 7x11-inch pan and dust with flour. Sift flour, baking powder, and salt together; set aside. Cream butter with sugar and add vanilla. Add eggs 1 at a time, beating well after each addition. By hand, add dry ingredients alternately with the milk. When smooth and blended, pour into prepared pans and bake about 25 minutes or until cake tests done with a cake tester. Cool 10 minutes; remove from pans and cool on a rack. Makes 2 thin layers.

SPONGE CAKE ROLL

Almost as versatile as a crêpe, this cake roll can be used with a wide range of fillings—everything from jelly to the most sophisticated cream.

     ¾ cup cake flour, sifted
     ¾ teaspoon baking powder
     ¼ teaspoon salt
     4 eggs
     ¾ cup sugar
     1 teaspoon vanilla
        Powdered sugar, sifted

Preheat oven to 375°. Line a 15½x10½x1-inch greased jelly roll pan with waxed paper; grease the paper. Sift flour, baking powder, and salt together; set aside. In a large bowl, beat eggs at high speed for 4 minutes or until thick. Gradually add the sugar. Beat at high speed until the mixture ribbons. Add vanilla. By hand, fold in the dry ingredients. Pour the batter into the prepared pan and bake for 12 minutes or until it tests done with a cake tester.

Sprinkle the top with powdered sugar; cover with a clean kitchen towel and then a board or heavy flat cardboard. Invert the pan onto the board, thus turning out the cake onto the towel. Carefully peel off the waxed paper. Trim off any crisp edges if necessary. Turn the edge of the towel over the cake and, beginning with the long side, roll the cake and towel together. Cool on rack. Unroll carefully and fill with your choice of fillings.

Dessert Toppings

CRÈME CHANTILLY

1 cup whipping cream, chilled
2 or more tablespoons powdered sugar, sifted
1 teaspoon vanilla or 1 tablespoon rum, brandy, or liqueur

Chill a mixing bowl and a whip or beaters. Beat the cream, slowly at first, increasing speed as it begins to thicken. Fold in the sugar and flavoring after the cream is whipped. Makes about 2 cups.

CRÈME FRAÎCHE

Use in finishing sauces as you would whipping cream. The butterfat content of at least 30 percent allows the cream to be simmered without curdling. To serve with desserts, add powdered sugar and optional flavoring.

1 cup whipping cream
   (not ultrapasteurized)
½ cup sour cream
1 tablespoon or more superfine sugar, optional
1 tablespoon Kirsch, optional

In a saucepan mix sour cream and whipping cream, combining with sugar and Kirsch, if desired. Heat gently only until mixture reaches room temperature. Cover loosely and keep at room temperature for 6 to 8 hours or overnight, until thickened. Refrigerate.

If time is a factor, a crème fraîche flavor dessert topping may be made. Lightly whip the cream until soft but not stiff. Gently fold in the sour cream and sugar and Kirsch, if desired. Mix only to blend. Makes 1½ cups.

MERINGUE

2 egg whites at room temperature
¼ teaspoon cream of tartar
   Dash salt
4 tablespoons sugar

Preheat oven to 350°. Beat egg whites slowly until frothy. Add cream of tartar and salt. Increase speed of beating until soft peaks form. Add sugar gradually, a little at a time. Beat until stiff, but not dry, and sugar is dissolved. If used for a pie topping, spread over the pie, being careful to seal meringue to the edges of the crust. Bake for 10 to 15 minutes, or until meringue is golden. Makes enough for one 9-inch pie.

PRALINE POWDER

A special finishing technique used particularly in French desserts. Sometimes gently folded into soufflés, cakes, or sauces to give a praline flavor and slight texture. Praline powder is also used in combination with butter to coat cake pans or mold.

1 cup sugar, caramelized (see Basics, page 188)
¼ cup almonds

Place almonds in a greased metal cake or pie tin. Very carefully pour the hot caramel over the nuts. Let harden. Remove from pan. Pound the sugar-almond mixture to a rather fine powder.

Dessert Sauces and Glazes

CARAMEL

Caramelizing occurs at a much higher temperature than that of boiling water. Handle with extreme caution.

Place 1 cup sugar in a very heavy cast iron skillet. Melt the sugar over medium heat, turning the skillet so that the sugar melts evenly. The sugar will turn golden brown. Remove the skillet from the fire just a few seconds before optimum color is achieved; heat from the skillet will continue to brown the sugar.

SIMPLE SYRUP

Simple sugar syrup has many uses in fine cooking. It can be flavored with liqueur and drizzled over cakes to add flavor and moisture. Use it to thin jams or preserves to a glaze or sauce consistency. Reversing the proportions (2 cups water to 1 cup sugar) produces a poaching liquid for fruits. Store leftover syrup in a tightly lidded jar, and it will keep almost indefinitely under refrigeration.

    2 cups sugar
    1 cup water
       Flavoring of your choice (1 teaspoon
       vanilla or 1 tablespoon of any liqueur)

Bring the sugar and water to a boil. Simmer until the sugar dissolves. Let cool briefly and add flavoring. Fruit juice or wine may be substituted for all or part of the water. If sweetened juice is used, adjust the amount of sugar to 1½ to 1¾ cups. Makes 1 cup.

APRICOT GLAZE

Add simple syrup (see Basics recipe above) to warm sieved apricot jam until the desired consistency is reached—about the thickness of corn syrup. Use this glaze on French-style tarts to give a finishing touch.

RED CURRANT GLAZE

Add simple syrup (see Basics recipe above) to warm red currant jelly. Thin to the desired consistency. Use this glaze on French-style tarts that require a rosy color, such as an apple tart.

APRICOT SAUCE

Thin warm apricot jam to sauce consistency with simple syrup (see Basics recipe above). Add brandy or liqueur to flavor, if desired. Serve with crêpes and beignets or a steaming soufflé.

RUM BUTTER SAUCE

Best served slightly warm over ice cream. Steamed raisins or chopped nuts may be added if desired.

    1 cup Simple Syrup (see Basics recipe above)
    4 tablespoons butter
    ¼ to ½ cup rum

Add butter to hot simple syrup. Cool slightly and add rum.

BERRY GLAZE FOR CHEESECAKES

½ cup berries (strawberries, blueberries, blackberries, etc.)
1 cup sugar
1 cup water
3 teaspoons arrowroot
¼ cup cold water
   Few drops food coloring, optional
   Additional berries to top the cake

Simmer berries with the sugar and water until the sugar is dissolved. Press through a sieve. Bring to a boil again and thicken to desired consistency with arrowroot dissolved in cold water. Add optional food coloring. Cool and pour over berries arranged on top of the cake. Let stand for 2 hours or more.

RASPBERRY SAUCE

1 pint fresh or 2 10-ounce packages frozen raspberries, thawed
   Sugar to taste
2 tablespoons Kirsch

Combine berries and sugar. Blend in food processor or blender. Strain and add Kirsch. Chill. Makes about 2 cups.

STRAWBERRY SAUCE

½ pint strawberries
   Sugar to taste
1 tablespoon or more Grand Marnier

Slice half the strawberries, crush the remainder and combine in a bowl. Gently mix in the sugar to taste. Add Grand Marnier. Chill. Makes about 1 cup.

CARAMEL SAUCE

A versatile dessert sauce that is excellent with profiteroles, cakes, and ice cream.

1¼ cups brown sugar
⅔   cup light corn syrup
4   tablespoons butter
¾   cup cream or evaporated milk

Cook brown sugar, corn syrup, and butter in a heavy pan to the soft ball stage stage (234°). Remove from heat and add cream. Stir well and return to heat for a few minutes. Do not allow to boil. Stir well before serving. Makes about 1½ cups.

BUTTERSCOTCH SAUCE

This rum-flavored sauce, similar to caramel sauce, is also suited to profiteroles, ice cream, and cakes.

1 cup brown sugar
½ cup canned evaporated milk
¼ cup butter
¼ cup rum

Bring brown sugar and milk to a boil. Add butter and boil 3 minutes. Cool and add rum. Makes about 1 cup.

CHOCOLATE SAUCE

A divine chocolate sauce. The perfect all-purpose sauce for chocolate lovers.

- 2 1-ounce squares unsweetened chocolate
- 1 cup sugar
-    Dash salt
- ⅓ cup whole milk
- 1 egg yolk, slightly beaten
- 1 teaspoon vanilla

In a double boiler, cook chocolate, sugar, salt, and milk until thick. Remove from heat and add egg yolk and vanilla. Makes about ¾ cup.

VANILLA SAUCE

This rich, luscious sauce is especially good for steamed puddings, chocolate cakes, angel cakes, and gingerbread.

- 5 tablespoons butter, melted
- 1 egg
- 1 cup powdered sugar, sifted
- 1 cup whipping cream, whipped
- 1 teaspoon vanilla

Combine butter and egg. Beat well and add sugar. Fold in whipped cream. Add flavoring. Makes about 2 cups.

Frostings and Fillings

MOCHA FROSTING

2 tablespoons strong coffee
1 tablespoon butter, melted
1 tablespoon coffee liqueur
1½ cups powdered sugar, sifted (variable)

Combine coffee, butter, and coffee liqueur. Add sifted sugar until frosting is of proper spreading consistency. Makes enough to frost one 7x11-inch cake or 14 éclairs.

CHOCOLATE FROSTING

A shiny chocolate frosting, just like Grandmother used to make, is especially good on my yellow cake. Top the cake with walnut halves.

2 1-ounce squares unsweetened chocolate
1 cup sugar
1 egg, beaten
3 tablespoons milk
2 tablespoons butter
Dash salt
½ teaspoon vanilla

Melt chocolate; add sugar, beaten egg, milk, butter, and salt. Cook over low flame until it comes to a good boil, stirring constantly. Remove and cool slightly. Add vanilla and beat until thick enough to spread. Makes enough to frost two 8-inch layers or one 9x13-inch cake.

CRÈME ANGLAISE

A basic vanilla-flavored custard sauce essential in French dessert cooking. It has many uses in combination with crêpes, puddings, and cakes.

3 egg yolks, slightly beaten
1 teaspoon flour
½ cup sugar
Dash salt
1½ cups milk, scalded
1 teaspoon vanilla

In the top of a double boiler, combine the egg yolks, flour, sugar, and salt. Gradually add the scalded milk. Cook over simmering water, stirring constantly, until the custard thickens slightly. Remove from heat; add vanilla. Stir occasionally as the custard cools to permit the steam to escape. Refrigerate to store. Makes 1½ cups.

PASTRY CREAM

A vanilla-flavored filling. The eggs in combination with the flour make a rich consistency, suitable as a filling for cakes, éclairs, and profiteroles.

½ cup sugar
¼ cup flour
4 egg yolks, lightly beaten
Dash salt
1½ cups milk, scalded
1 teaspoon vanilla

In the top of a double boiler, combine sugar, flour, egg yolks, and salt. Slowly add the scalded milk. Mix well and cook over simmering water until mixture thickens, about 10 minutes. Cool, stirring occasionally. Add vanilla. Store in refrigerator. Makes 1½ cups.

QUICK PASTRY CREAM

Prepare any name brand pudding mix, using 1¾ cups milk instead of 2 cups. Add 1 tablespoon brandy or your own choice natural flavor to counteract the artificial flavor in the mix. Makes about 2 cups.

MOCHA CREAM

A coffee-flavored filling, especially delicious in éclairs.

    ¾ cup sugar
    ⅓ cup flour, sifted
       Dash salt
    2 cups milk, scalded and mixed with 3
       tablespoons instant coffee
    2 egg yolks, lightly beaten
    2 tablespoons coffee liqueur

Combine the sugar, flour, and salt in the top of a double boiler. Gradually blend in the milk and coffee mixture with a whisk. Cook over simmering water until thick. Stir a small amount of this mixture into the egg yolks; then beat the yolks into the hot mixture and cook briefly until smooth and thick. Cool; add liqueur. Store in refrigerator. Makes 2 cups.

LEMON CURD

This marvelous lemon-sweet filling or spread can be used as a filling for layer cakes, cake rolls, pies, sweet rolls, and as a spread for hot breads and toasts. For filling or topping, use as is or fold in ½ cup or more whipped cream to lighten. For lemon sauce, heat in a double boiler, add about ¼ cup boiling water, and whisk to blend. Keeps well in the refrigerator for up to 3 weeks.

    2 cups sugar
    4 eggs, lightly beaten
       Dash salt
       Juice of 2 lemons
    2 tablespoons butter

In a double boiler, combine sugar, eggs, salt, and lemon juice. Cook over simmering water until very thick, whisking constantly. Remove from heat and stir in butter. Chill. Makes about 2½ cups curd, enough for one 8-inch pie.

Index

Order *Verna Meyer's Menu Cookbook* from your bookstore, or send a check for $10.95 plus $.75 for postage and handling to

Dillon Press, Inc.
500 South Third Street
Minneapolis, Minnesota 55415